OSPREY AIRCRAFT OF THE ACES • 21

Polish Aces of World War 2

SERIES EDITOR: TONY HOLMES

OSPREY AIRCRAFT OF THE ACES • 21

Polish Aces of World War 2

Robert Gretzyngier and Wojtek Matusiak

Front cover
The Mustang III of Sqn Ldr Eugeniusz 'Dziubek' Horbaczewski, OC No 315 Sqn, is depicted during the air combat of 30 July 1944 in which six aircraft from the unit downed eight German fighters off the Norwegian coast. Horbaczewski's report from that combat read as follows;

'While escorting Beaufighters over the Norwegian coast on July 30th at 1555 hrs we met about 15 ME 109s and attacked them. We were above them and the MEs were apparently not expecting to see single-engined fighters so far north, as they took no evasive action, possibly mistaking us for other ME 109s. I dived down on them and gave one a three-second burst, after which he caught fire and went straight into the sea. I climbed up, and when climbing I spotted another ME 109 below me. I came down and gave him a long burst. Strikes were seen in the cockpit and on the wings, glycol began to leak from the enemy aircraft and it was losing speed and height. My guns jammed so I formated on him and started calling by R/T my No 2 (Flg Off Bożydar Nowosielski). The enemy aircraft had no hood and I could see that the pilot's face was covered in blood and he put up his hands.

'He was heading towards the Norwegian coast, so I ordered my No 2 to open fire. After two bursts my No 2 overshot him, and the enemy aircraft went into the sea. When last seen, the pilot was adjusting his "Mae West". I claim 1 1/2 ME 109s destroyed.'

Horbaczewski was flying his normal mount – FB166/PK-G – on this mission (see profile 43 for more details). It is believed that by late July, the number of bombing mission symbols had grown, and four V1 kill markings had also appeared under the canopy (*Cover artwork by Iain Wyllie*)

Previous pages
PZL P.11c 'White 10' (serial 8.70) of *113 Eskadra* is seen during a training scramble. On 1 September 1939 the aeroplane was seriously damaged, but was repaired and is shown in its later guise in profile 1 (*Kopański*)

First published in Great Britain in 1998
by Osprey Publishing
Michelin House, 81 Fulham Road,
London SW3 6RB

ISBN 1 85532726 0

Edited by Tony Holmes
Page design by TT Designs, T & S Truscott
Cover Artwork by Iain Wyllie
Aircraft Profiles by Robert Gretzyngier and Robert 'Buba' Grudzień
Figure Artwork by Mike Chappell
Scale Drawings by Robert Gretzyngier

Printed in Hong Kong

Authors' Note
The authors would like to hear from persons involved with Polish Air Force fighter pilots during the World War 2 period, as well as owners of associated documentation and photographs. Please write to Wojtek Matusiak, s.p. 35, 00-987 Warszawa 4, Poland.

CONTENTS

THE LAST AND THE FIRST

On 25 April 1945 at about 1900 hrs, whilst flying Yak-9M 'white 87' (serial 3215387), ppor. Viktor Kalinovski shot down an Fw 190 about eight kilometres west of Friesack (40 km north-west of Berlin). This was the pilot's 12th aerial victory, and the last kill credited to any Polish Air Force (PAF) ace in World War 2.

The so called 'People's Polish Army' (organised with Stalin's encouragement after he had broken off diplomatic relations with the legal Polish government) had four fighter regiments. These units entered combat in late 1944 and had scored less than 20 victories by war's end, this total including two by Kalinovski, who was the formation's sole ace. The PAF's final kill of the war offered an ominous portent of things to come, for Kalinovski was not a Pole at all, rather one of the many Soviet officers posted to man the hastily-formed Polish units – although a substantial number of Polish officers had been captured by the Soviets in the wake of the 1939 invasion, few were still alive by this late stage in the war. He would soon return to his country.

The name of Kalinovski's unit – *1 Pułk Lotnictwa Myśliwskiego 'Warszawa'* (1st Fighter Aviation Regiment 'Warsaw') – implied a connection with the pre-war Warsaw-based *1 Pułk Lotniczy* (1st Air Regiment). In a ironic twist to this final victory, it had been an officer of the latter unit – ppor. Witold Urbanowicz – who had scored the first kill accredited to a future Polish ace some nine years before when he had shot down a Soviet aeroplane!

In August 1936 a Soviet military aircraft had entered Polish airspace (like many before) and refused to turn back, in spite of signals from intercepting Polish fighters. Young Urbanowicz, unable to stand such provocative behaviour any longer, swiftly sent the intruder down. However, Urbanowicz's superiors did not consider his actions to be a civilised way of settling such incidents, and the pilot soon had to say goodbye to his unit, the most distinguished and renowned *Eskadra Kościuszkowska*. He was posted to undertake instructor duties at *Szkoła Podchorążych Lotnictwa* (Polish Air Force college) at Dęblin, where it was hoped his energies would find better outlet, and his skills transferred to many a young pilot.

INTO BATTLE

As the summer of 1939 wore on, the political situation in Europe left few doubts in most peoples' minds that war was imminent. On 23 August the Polish Air Force (PAF) was re-organised into a wartime structure, which meant disbanding Air Regiments at their permanent bases and deploying individual *Eskadras* according to a preplanned scheme. *Brygada Pościgowa* (Pursuit Brigade) was formed for the air defence of Warsaw, incorporating four *Eskadras* from *Zgrupowanie Myśliwskie* (Fighter Group) of *1 Pułk Lotniczy*, plus *123 Eskadra* from Cracow. The remaining fighter units were assigned to land armies, in accordance with the prevailing concept of strict co-operation with ground troops – the Order of Battle for Polish fighter units both before and after the re-organisation is given in the appendices.

In anticipation of the German attack, virtually every combat unit moved from their peace-time base to an advanced landing ground. Between 24 and 31 August all fighter *Eskadras* moved to small airfields, some changing their temporary bases several times during that week.

As a result of this movement, when German bombers struck at principal PAF bases on the morning of 1 September 1939, all they hit in terms of aircraft were some unserviceable machines, leaving the entire Polish fighter force intact to oppose the Luftwaffe. However, despite having survived the first round of bombings, the PAF was given little chance of prevailing against the superior German aircraft by outside observers. Polish P.11s had already encountered Dornier Do 17 reconnaissance aircraft

American volunteers Merian C Cooper (left) and Cedric E Fauntleroy set up a whole US-manned unit – known as the *Eskadra Kościuszkowska* (Kościuszko Squadron) – to fight in the Polish-Bolshevik war of 1920. The unit's badge comprised US stars and stripes with a superimposed Polish peasant's hat and scythes prepared for fighting. The latter elements were emblems of the anti-Russian uprising of 1794, led by Gen Kościuszko. As he had also been a general in the American War of Independence, Kościuszko made a perfect patron for Polish-American brotherhood-in-arms (*Kopański*)

The Polish designed and built PWS-26 was the principal training type used by would-be fighter pilots at Dęblin. The aircraft was also used for practicing blind flying techniques (*Kopański*)

before the war, learning that the latter flew too high and too fast to be intercepted. This scenario was repeated many times during the campaign, as air defence sites would detect German raids and scramble fighters to intercept them, only for the latter to find that they were unable to catch the attackers. It was whilst attempting to engage the numerous German bomber formations that the outclassed P.11 units suffered their first losses. This uneven struggle favoured the tactics oriented towards fighter-v-fighter combat, and early recognition of the approaching enemy. Thus, Polish fighter pilots were the first amongst the Allies to fly both in pairs and in loose squadron formations.

The first week of fighting saw numerous heavy air battles take place, and it is now generally accepted that the first kill of World War 2 was that achieved by a Ju 87 pilot at Cracow (see *Osprey Combat Aircraft 1 - Ju 87 Stukageschwader 1937-41* for more details) when he shot down a P.11c taking off. Minutes later ppor. Władysław Gnyś destroyed two Do 17s. These early actions served as mere precursors for the 'main event', which occurred in the vicinity of Warsaw at about 0715 when some 35 He 111Ps of II.(L)/LG 1 (led by Hauptmann Alfred Bülowius), escorted by

Great importance was attached to the general fitness of cadet officers at the Polish Air Force college. Here, instructor por. Witold Urbanowicz leads a line of his cadets during routine skiing training. Right behind him is Stanisław Juszczak (later killed with No 303 Sqn), followed by Stanisław Bochniak (who was commanding 'A' Flight of No 308 Sqn at war's end), unidentified, Bolesław Kaczmarek (OC No 302 Sqn at war's end, and later killed in a Pakistani jet fighter in the 1950s) and 'Dziubek' Horbaczewski. These cadets were from the 13th Promotion, which was the last class of the Dęblin College commissioned before the war commenced . In the official PAF aces' listing, Urbanowicz ranks second and Horbaczewski third (*Bochniak*)

Fighters of *111 Eskadra*. This unit inherited the *Kościuszko* tradition, and continued to use the 1920-vintage badge. In this view (probably taken during the weeks prior to the outbreak of war), 'White 5' and '1' are P.11cs, while the remaining aircraft are older P.11as (*Kopański*)

24 Bf 110Cs of I.(Z)/LG 1 (led by Major Walter Grabmann), were intercepted by P.11s of *Brygada Pościgowa*. The first kill was shared by por. Aleksander Gabszewicz and kpr. Andrzej Niewiara, who jointly destroyed a Heinkel (Gabszewicz later acquired parts of its fin as his trophy). Their success was soon emulated by other pilots including kpt. Adam Kowalczyk (OC *IV/1 Dywizjon*) and por. Hieronim Dudwal (of *113 Eskadra*), both of whom destroyed He 111s, and who would eventually feature among the top-scorers of the doomed 1939 campaign. The same combat also saw ppor. Łokuciewski credited with a shared probable – a score to which he would add a further eight kills during the war.

Four more aces opened their accounts on the first day of what nobody yet expected to become a world war. During his two sorties, kpr. Jan Kremski of *121 Eskadra* was credited with a He 111 destroyed and a Henschel Hs 126 shared destroyed, whilst in the afternoon por. Marian Pisarek destroyed a Hs 126, which he shared with fellow *141 Eskadra* pilot kpr. Mielczyński. The German reconnaissance aeroplane force-landed in a field, and was followed down by ppor. Stanisław Skalski (of *142 Eskadra*), who landed his P.11c nearby in order to capture German maps and documents before the Henschel's crew could destroy them. During the afternoon raid on Warsaw, ppor. Radomski (*113 Eskadra*) was credited with a Bf 109 destroyed. In the same combat por. Gabszewicz was shot down, thus becoming the first of the future Polish aces to take to his parachute during the war. Kpr. Cwynar of *113 Eskadra* was also credited with destroying an unidentified enemy aircraft during the Warsaw raid.

Over the next five days no less than twelve Polish aces opened their scores in the heavy fighting – ppor. Ferić and plut. Karubin of *111 Eskadra*, por. Łapkowski (*112*), st. szer. Adamek (*113*), ppor. Nowak and ppor. Król (both *121*), ppor. Własnowolski (*122*), ppor. Pniak (*142*),

Pilots of *3 Pułk Lotniczy* exercise their tactical skills during a model combat simulation (*Kopański*)

kpr. Bełc (*152*), ppor. Koc (*161*), ppor. Główczyński (*162*) and kpt. Szczęsny. The last pilot in this list had been a flying instructor until the outbreak of war, when he joined an ad-hoc air defence squadron manned by the Ułęż-based *Szkoła Wyższego Pilotażu* (Advanced Flying School) instructors. The unit claimed two probables or damaged on 2 September flying P.7as, which were considered even more obsolete than the P.11! By 4 September ppor. Skalski of *142 Eskadra* had been credited with four and one shared kills, thus becoming the first Allied ace of World War 2.

After the first week of action in the immediate wake of the invasion, the intensity of air combat decreased as less and less Polish aircraft could be made serviceable and the advance of German ground troops forced *Eskadras* to withdraw east. Nevertheless, it was between 8 and 13 September that mjr Mümler, OC *III/2 Dywizjon*, was credited with two and two shared kills. On 14 and 15 September 'Hesio' Szczęsny

Casually-attired flying personnel of *III/6 Dywizjon* receive orders on 31 August 1939. Like virtually every combat unit of the Polish Air Force, they had moved to a camouflaged forward landing ground, leaving peace-time bases empty for *Luftwaffe* strikes the next morning. The aircraft seen in front of the P.11 fighters parked in the background is an RWD-8 trainer (still wearing its civil registration), which had been requisitioned from a flying club just prior to the outbreak of war. These machines would be used extensively for liaison duties virtually until the end of the Polish campaign in October 1939 (*Główczyński*)

claimed the only confirmed kills credited to the Ulęż instructors' unit following his 'acquisition' of the prototype P.11g fighter, evacuated from the PZL works. This aircraft was a substantially improved version of the P.11, and Szczęsny demonstrated its potency by downing two He 111s.

Enter Stalin

By mid-September a major part of the Polish fighter force was assembled in the south-eastern part of the country near the border with Rumania – Poland's neighbour at that time. Promised deliveries of weapons from the West (including Hurricanes and MS.406s) were expected to arrive any day now, being directed to Rumanian ports on the Black Sea following the German capture of the Baltic ports .

As the Polish Army was retreating east, the situation seemed less disastrous for the beleaguered defenders, for eastern Poland was covered with forests and marshes that would render the enemy's *Panzerwaffe* virtually useless. This area would favour infantry and cavalry, which prevailed in the Polish army. As proved later by the Soviet-Finnish wars, defence of such territory could have been very effective . . .

However, on 17 September the Soviet Red Army invaded Poland to make sure that no such defence would be possible, and although the war on two fronts would continue until October, it was on thus day that

Mjr Mieczysław Mümler, OC *III/3 Dywizjon*, is seen with his pilots. Mümler was one of the top scorers of the 1939 campaign, being credited with two and two shared German aircraft destroyed. He would score a kill and a shared over France during June 1940, followed by a further victory during the Battle of Britain (*Kopański*)

The PZL P.7a fighter was obsolete even compared to the P.11c, and although underpowered and underarmed, it was used with some success by pilots of several *Eskadras* that were still equipped with the type in 1939. This particular machine was in service with the Advanced Flying School at Ulęż (the code letter 'U' can just be made out to the right of the underwing PAF marking) (*Wandzilak*)

Camouflaged P.11 fighters and their pilots at Młynów airfield in mid-September 1939. Note that by this stage in the invasion all unit emblems and code numbers had been hastily painted out to make the aircraft less conspicuous on the ground. Third from right is kpr. Michał Cwynar, whilst at far right is st. szer. Mieczysław Adamek – both pilots scored their first kills with *113 Eskadra* in 1939, before later becoming aces with the RAF (*Cwynar*)

Poland was truly defeated. With the conflict now being fought on two fronts, major units had to be careful not to be encircled by the advancing Soviet forces. Aerial reconnaissance became more crucial than ever in determining where the enemy was, and as the Luftwaffe had effectively secured control of the skies, these missions were flown principally by P.11 fighters, which stood the best chance of survival. During such sorties on 17 September a number of Soviet aircraft were destroyed or damaged – ppor. Tadeusz Koc of *161 Eskadra* became the only future Polish ace to be credited with the destruction of a communist aircraft when he shot down a Polikarpov R-5 reconnaissance aeroplane on this date. The following day PAF units were ordered to fly across the border to Rumania when it became obvious that Soviet troops were on the verge of capturing the airfields they were operating from.

Small aerial support units continued to operate in eastern Poland right up until the end of the armed struggle, however. Interestingly, these flights were not only Polish-manned, for after the partition of Czechoslovakia, a group of Czech aviators had fled to Poland in an effort to continue flying. These pilots were viewed with some suspicion by the Polish authorities (similar to how the Poles were later treated in the West), and it eventually took the invasion to change the high command's viewpoint.

When the Czechs were finally formed into a regular flying unit, their first duty was to participate in the defence against Stalin's invasion. They soldiered on, inflicting losses on Red Army units before escaping to Rumania at the end of September. As Czech authorities in exile were careful to maintain friendly relations with the USSR, these pilots initially stuck to PAF units in the West, rather than creating autonomous Czech-manned squadrons. Among those who chose to stay with the Poles even after Czech squadrons had been formed in Britain was Josef Frantisek, who would later become a Hurricane ace (see *Osprey Aircraft of the Aces 18 - Hurricane Aces 1939-40* for further details).

SIKORSKI'S TOURISTS

Following the collapse of Polish resistance in the face of overwhelming odds, most surviving PAF fighter pilots of all ranks managed to enter neutral Rumania or Hungary. Here, they were initially interned, but bribery or persuasion soon turned them into 'students', 'artists' and other 'tourists', thus allowing them to travel on. Following Gen Sikorski's (new C-in-C Polish Armed Forces) orders, they headed for France – most by ship from Rumanian, Yugoslav or Greek ports, via Syria, Lebanon or Malta, although some went overland through Italy.

Few Polish airmen were captured by the Germans, for most of those who stayed under Nazi occupation managed to revert to being simple 'civilians'. Later, many would travel illegally across the Tatra mountains to Slovakia, thence to Hungary or Rumania, and along the routes described above. Others stayed in Poland and joined the underground Home Army. Of those who surrendered in the Soviet-held territory, a few were able to escape through Baltic and Scandinavian countries to fight on. Those not so lucky soon found themselves in *gulags*, where many perished along with hundreds of thousands of their compatriots – most of the officers (including PAF personnel) met their sad end in mass executions.

For those that had escaped, late 1939 and early 1940 saw increasing numbers of them arriving in France, and by April no less than 8500 airmen had made it to the West. There, they found a nation gripped by the spell of the 'Phoney War', encountering many peace-minded Frenchmen who considered the Poles responsible for the outbreak of hostilities!

Having received a less than warm welcome from their Allies, the Polish airmen assembled at the main training centre in Lyon, organised by plk Stefan Pawlikowski, who was well known in France for his exploits as a fighter pilot during World War 1. Pawlikowski was influential in gaining

During conversion training in France Polish pilots flew a mixture of types, including the North American NAA.57Et2, which was the predecessor of the T-6 Texan/Harvard (*Wandzilak*)

The Morane-Saunier MS.406C1 was by far the most widely used Allied fighter type of the Battle of France. This aeroplane was photographed at Lyon-Bron airfield, which served as the main base for the Polish Air Force in France. Note the Polish-marked twin-engined Caudron Goeland taking-off in the background (*Wandzilak*)

the support of French pilots from the Great War, the latter individuals duly proving helpful during the formation of the Polish centre – and subsequently during the evacuation panic of a few months later. Many Polish pilots started to polish up their French (which many of them already spoke fluently), whilst others volunteered for single-engined bomber training in Britain. Some fighter pilots who saw no prospect of operational flying in France also headed for the UK. Most, however, stayed in France, where the first group started conversion onto Morane-Saulnier MS.406s in early 1940. On 7 January 1940 20 pilots were sent to *Centre d'Instruction d'Aviation de Chasse* at Montpellier for conversion.

On 17 February *Accord Technique Relatif a la Constitution des Forces Aeriennes Polonaises en France* was signed, thus allowing for the potential re-creation of the PAF, underpinned by French technical support – hope now returned to the air force personnel, who had spent the cold winter in unheated barracks at Lyon. By now the first group of pilots had also completed their training and returned as instructors to teach others. Two more groups were established at Lyon-Bron airfield under mjr Kępiński and mjr Pamula, respectively. In all, more than 70 pilots would be trained on MS.406s in 1940. Capitaine (now General) Pierre Rougevin-Baville was responsible for the training of Polish pilots, and he later recalled;

'As soon as I evaluated them in the air, I understood they had little to learn about air combat – some had already scored victories in Poland. All that was necessary was for them to acquaint themselves with the MS.406, plus introduce them to our formations, signalling and other routines.'

The Montpellier group finished training in late March, and on the 27th Lyon-Bron was visited by Polish and French officials who took part in the ceremonial assignment of personnel to French units. Pilots of the *'Groupe Montpellier'* (Montpellier Squadron) were split into sections and attached to French units – *Groupe de Chasse* (GC) III/1, I/2, III/2, II/6, III/6 and II/7. Each section (with a team of Polish groundcrew) had three brand new MS.406s adorned with Polish markings on the fuselage.

Por. Kazimierz Bursztyn's section, which was attached to GC III/1 *Le Renard Clignotant* (Winking Fox), included ppor. Gnyś who, following the subsequent German attack on the Low Countries, shared in the destruction of a He 111 over Belgium on 12 May 1940 – he was credited with shared kills over two Do 17s four days later, thus making him the first Polish pilot to become an ace during the French campaign.

Despite Gnyś's success, the section attached to GC II/7 would eventually become the most successful *Patrouille polonaise* of the Battle of France. Amongst its pilots were por. Władysław Goethel (the GC's OC), ppor. Król and kpr. Nowakiewicz, supported by three fitters, one armourer, one electrician, three support technicians and three soldiers.

The *Patrouille polonaise* first encountered enemy aircraft on 2 May 1940 when Goethel and Nowakiewicz shot up a He 111. Some time after this action, ppłk pil. Mümler joined GC II/7 directly from the Bron training centre following the dispersal of his last group of student pilots to other frontline French fighter units.

Although various wartime documents give vastly differing accounts of the Polish section's combats with GC II/7, two actions do stand out. During the late afternoon of 1 June 1940 ppłk Mümler shot down a He 111 near the Swiss border under the watchful eye of that country's fighter section. He also claimed a second He 111 shared with French fighters of GC II/7 during the mission, but never received confirmation for this kill.

The Polish section's last action (on 15 June) was described by Mümler; 'I was in the section led by sous-lieutenant Valentin, with kpr. Nowakiewicz. After some time in our area we encountered a group of Do 17s. We broke their formation immediately, and I chose one for myself. My first attack was successful, as I noticed two crew members leave the plane and open parachutes. I passed very close to them, and could see horror on their faces. I watched the Dornier until it crashed, while keeping an eye on the parachutes. I also noticed another Dornier attacked by a Dewoitine (D.520) at low level. It was Nowakiewicz. We attacked this bomber twice, but the German was flying just above the ground and it was difficult to aim, especially as the rear gunner defended himself stubbornly. Nowakiewicz quit and went home, but I was anxious to finish it.

'After another attack I was sure it was over. It was then that I felt I was

Groupe Montpellier was essentially a Polish fighter squadron that was split into separate sections and assigned to French units. Each of the latter squadrons sent a three-aircraft section to Lyon on 27 March 1940 for a ceremony which welcomed the newly-trained Polish pilots into the *Armée de l'Air*. The three MS.406s seen in the foreground of this photograph were assigned to GC III/1. No 1031 (nearest the camera) was flown by por. Bursztyn, whilst the aircraft parked next to it (No 936) was assigned to ppor. Gnyś – the latter pilot subsequently became the first Polish ace of the Battle of France (*SHAA via Zaleski*)

GC III/1's Por. Kazimierz Bursztyn (right) relaxes with his Polish groundcrew between flights. His MS.406 – 'White I' – was numbered 1031 (*Koniarek*)

hit, but I do not know if it was the gunner or ground fire. My Dewoitine was fully controllable, but glycol was spattering on the windshield. It was no joke – the engine could seize at any moment. I turned south. When I approached the town of Langres, oil temperature rose and the engine started to shake. My altitude was 1000 m and I was looking for a place to land. It seemed strange that there was no movement on the roads below. I saw smoke over the town of Grey, it looked like it had been bombed not long before. My engine refused to work completely. I was some 12 kms away from the airfield. I had to fly over a forest, cross a river, and touch down. My aeroplane was losing altitude and speed. I saw the river. I could land on either bank, but thought it reasonable to land on the east. I saw a slightly ascending field. I extended the undercarriage and flaps, turned ignition off, and landed. I stopped just in front of a forest. The engine was steaming like a teapot. Before I jumped out of the cockpit, I heard artillery grenades nearby. With no time even to unstrap the parachute harness, I ran to the forest. Here, I met a French soldier who told me that the Germans were right across the river.'

By the time of the French surrender, the Polish pilots of GC II/7 had achieved the following scores – kpr. Nowakiewicz (Polish top-scorer of the Battle of France), 3 and 2 shared kills; ppor. Król, 2 kills and 1 probable; ppłk Mümler, 1 and 1 shared kill, plus 1 shared damaged; and por. Goethel, 1 kill (unconfirmed by Polish authorities).

Por. Józef Brzeziński's section, attached to GC I/2 *Cicognes* (Storks), had also distinguished itself during the struggle for France, with ppor. Chałupa emerging as its most successful pilot. In the campaign's initial weeks, GC I/2's airfields at Xaffevilliers and Ochey had twice been bombed by the Germans, with the attack on 27 May costing the unit almost all of its MS.406s. Prior to these devastating raids, Chałupa, along with plut. Antoni Beda, had shot at a Ju 88 bomber on 11 May, which had escaped trailing black smoke. Six days later the former pilot force landed with a burning engine and was subsequently taken to a hospital. However, by the 21st he was back with his unit.

On 5 June GC I/2's *Patrouille polonaise* (which had made good its losses of 27 May with ex-GC II/7 MS.406) intercepted a lone Ju 88 northwest of Clairvaux, ppor. Chałupa and plut. Beda (along with a French pilot) swiftly downing the intruder – this victory was the first confirmed kill for GC I/2's *Patrouille polonaise.* Three days later the unit engaged a large formation of twin-engined bombers, escorted by Bf 109s. In the ensuing battle, nine enemy aircraft were reported to have been shot down, with ppor. Chałupa claiming a single Bf 109 destroyed. Later that same afternoon the Polish pilot intercepted two Ju 87s over Beauvais and Soissons, shooting one of the dive-bombers down himself and sharing in the destruction of the second with two French pilots.

Finland's Squadron

In late November 1939 the Soviet Union invaded Finland, and whilst France and Britain began forming Expeditionary Forces, the Polish government in exile was also invited to join the fight against the Soviet Union as, of course, the latter had been at war with Poland since 17 September. Preparations for war on the Soviet-Finnish front proceeded apace, with the formation of a Polish squadron (commanded by mjr. Józef Kępinski) equipped with MS.406s at Lyon Bron – this solitary unit was to be part of a multi-national force to be despatched from Western Europe. Aside from MS.406s, Caudron-Renault C.714 Cyclones were also issued to the Poles, as both types had previously been exported to Finland.

However, before the Polish unit could complete its formation, the Finns unexpectedly signed a ceasefire with the Soviet Union on 12 March 1940 – 'Finland's Squadron' subsequently became the *Groupe de Chasse Polonaise de Varsovie* I/145 on 6 April 1940. Two days after the German invasion, GC I/145 was ordered to convert entirely to the CR.714. Accordingly, on 18 May pilots went to Villacoublay to collect their new aeroplanes, but were disappointed to find that although the Caudron was an excellent flying 'toy' (it had been developed from the *Coupe Deutsch de la Meurthe* racers of the mid-1930s), it was useless for combat – the *Armée de l'Air* had already declared the aircraft unsuitable for its fighter units.

At that point production Cyclones were still suffering teething troubles, and a team of factory engineers was duly assigned to the Polish unit in an attempt to correct the aircraft's thoroughly unreliable hydraulic system and propeller pitch mechanism. Despite the engineers' best efforts, malfunctions grounded so many CR.714s that the French authorities banned further training on the type. However, by that stage the Battle of France was in full swing, and mjr Kępiński did not want to wait for the promised Bloch MB 152 replacements to arrive – he ordered to the conversion to be completed. By 27 May GC I/145 was fully operational, with its two flights of CR 714s ready to fight.

On 2 June the unit moved to Dreux, and six days later they encountered a formation of Bf 110s, downing five of them – two fell victim to por. Czerwiński (one of the unit's most successful aviators). GC I/145's por. Główczyński became a hero the following morning (9 June) when he was credited with a Bf 109 destroyed and two probable kills. Before this sortie, ppor. Jerzy Czerniak – Główczyński's wingman – had promised to protect the latter's tail. He later described this action;

'We came a bit into the sun, and "Czesiek" (Główczyński) attacked, while I followed him as his fan. I uncocked my guns, just in case, as you never know what the Messerschmitts will want to do. This proved quite useful as, would you believe, when we jumped in the middle of them, and "Czesiek" unceremoniously got on one's tail, the others got after him, paying no attention to me. I kept on waiting for the action to develop. "Czesiek" was firing at his victim, who tried every trick to escape, but in vain. I was following "Czesiek" all the time, and paid special attention to one Messerschmitt which decided to take my friend's life. When its rudeness became dangerous I decided to put an end to that show. The Messerschmitt attacked "Czesiek" from behind, and even fired a burst, when I jumped on it and sent a nice portion into the cockpit. Evidently this was

Prior to joining the *Armée de l'Air*, Ppor. Władysław Gnyś had been the first Polish (and Allied) pilot to shoot down a German aircraft on the morning of 1 September 1939. He was also the second Polish pilot to become an ace when he shared in the destruction of a Do 17 over Belgium on 16 May 1940
(*SHAA via Zaleski*)

Por. Dudwał was credited with four kills in 1939 before fleeing Poland for France. Following his conversion onto the MS.406, Dudwał was posted to the Polish section of GC II/10, but was killed during its first combat on 7 June 1940. During the engagement a number of Bf 109s were also destroyed, although the French unit actually claimed fewer than was subsequently admitted lost by the Luftwaffe. Therefore, it is possible that Dudwał may have achieved 'acedom' in the minutes prior to his death (*Pawlak*)

Although the Caudron-Renault CR.714 Cyclone was a joy to fly, it was virtually useless in combat. Nevertheless, Polish-manned GC I/145 took the type into action in early June 1940 (the only unit to do so) and scored a number of victories with it

well aimed, as he turned his mount on its back immediately. I gave him another, and the "Me" decided to withdraw from the combat, but it was too late. I did not let "my friend" go, until he fell down in the form of a "petite souvenir" in a French farmer's back yard. After the combat I meet "Czesiek", and it turns out that he also finished off his Me.'

The Bf 109s crashed south of Andelys. This was Główczyński's fifth kill, for he had already claimed three and one shared destroyed in 1939.

A total of four Bf 109s and three Do 17s were confirmed destroyed on 9 and 10 June, for the loss of three pilots and seven CR.714s. On the latter date the unit moved to Sermaises, and three days later to Chateauroux-La Martinerie, where they received three MB.152s. Sixteen pilots were assigned to GC I/1 and I/8 at Rochefort, with GC I/145 moving there on 17 June. The following day kpt. Wczelik and plut. Markiewicz downed a He 111 over the sea, which subsequently proved to be the last Allied air victory of the Battle of France. That evening the squadron abandoned its remaining Caudrons and two MB.152s at Rochefort, and on 19 June the airmen embarked on a ship at La Rochelle, bound for Britain .

A chronic shortage of aircraft (all available fighters had been issued to frontline units) saw pilots of the 3rd and 4th Polish Squadrons forced to form nine sections that were duly assigned to French fighter units in mid-May, rather than operating autonomously like the Montpellier Squadron and GC I/145. Other Bron graduates would protect 11 main bases, factories and industrial centres in small units called *ELD* (*Escadrille Legere de Defence* – Light Defence Flight) or *ECD* (*Escadrille de Chasse et de Defence* – Fighter and Defence Flight) – nicknamed 'Chimney Flights'.

The busiest of these was the flight at Romorantin under kpt. Tadeusz Opulski, who, like most of his pilots (including por. Łapkowski and ppor. Łokuciewski), had been credited with victories during the 1939 campaign. Whilst defending the Morane-Saulnier assembly line, and Koolhoven FK.58 and MS.406 depots, they added a total of six kills and two probables to their scores. Another successful 'Chimney Flight' was the one in defence of the Curtiss Hawk 75 assembly line at Bourges, which was led by kpt. Kosiński and included por. Wesołowski, plut. Pietrasiak and kpr. Kremski – they downed four He 111s and damaged four more.

As France was about to collapse, Polish 'Chimney Flight' pilots flew many different types of aircraft, with Mjr Krasnodębski's ECD I/55 section (flying in defence of Etampes) using FK.58s, MS.406s and MB. 152s. Ppor. Zumbach later wrote;

'I went to a new airfield – Villacoublay, near Paris – together with Zdzisław (Krasnodębski) on 10 June. It took us some seven hours to cover 50 km due to crowded roads. On 11 June we started flying in defence of Paris. Communication was already interrupted and we usually took off on the sound of enemy planes. It was there that we received new aeroplanes – Arsenal VGs – beautiful in shape and performances. After two days of fruitless

Exotic foreign types were not only used as trainers, for the Dutch Koolhoven FK.58C1 fighter was also flown – and disliked – by several Polish pilots, including future ace Jan Falkowski, who commanded the Polish flight at Cognac (*Wandzilak*)

mid-air chases, there came an uproar that the "Jerries" were only a few kilometres away. It was 13 June. That night, during a terrible thunderstorm, we evacuated to Etampes. I took a Curtiss and an Arsenal. Zdzisław took a Morane 410. The following day we were flying from Etampes, patrolling the Paris-Orlean road, because every now and then the "Hun" would appear, strafing and bombing the road, and raising panic.'

More than 130 Polish fighter pilots flew operationally during the Battle of France. They were credited with the destruction of 60 aircraft for the loss of 13 killed in combat, or due to German bombing and strafing.

Following the French surrender on 18 June, Gen Sikorski ordered every Polish soldier to evacuate to Britain. However, this was no easy task for fighter pilots attached to French units on the front, or for large groups of student pilots in training centres. Most moved south with their units and, after disbandment, headed for Port Vendres, Marseille or Biarritz to board ships. Many flew to Africa where, on the last drops of fuel, they would reach Oran and Tunis in their Hawks, MB.152s, MS.406s, D.520s, small transports and requisitioned private aircraft. From there they would go by sea, via Gibraltar, to Britain.

The only Polish unit which arrived in Britain with its aircraft was the Chateauroux 'Chimney Flight' of por. Henneberg. He later reported;

'After I received information that Germans were near Bourges (60 km from Chateauroux), I decided to move to Bordeaux with all personnel. At 1900 entire flight took off: one Bloch 152, two Bloch 151s and one Caudron-Simoun, crewed by ppor. Wielgus and pchor. Pokrzywka. Bloch 151s were flown by ppor. Witold Retinger and ppor. Bruno Kudrewicz. When we came to Bordeaux, where I received information that first groups of Polish airmen were already waiting in harbour for evacuation, I decided to fly to England. On 18 June at 0830 entire section took off from Burdeaux and landed at Nantes about 1000. At Nantes I addressed an RAF wing commander, whom I did not know, with the question of if we could fly to England? I received affirmative answer, directions to Tangmere airfield, and a letter to the Station HQ there. After refuelling, we left Nantes at 1400. At 1630 we landed at Tangmere, and three hours later we were moved to Andover. The following afternoon I was ordered to fly with my flight to Netheravon, where we left the French aircraft.'

For most Polish pilots the French episode ended just as it had started – on a ship. The object of their journey this time was the 'Last Hope Island'. The 'tourism' was about to end, however, for there was nowhere left to go.

BATTLE FOR BRITAIN

As briefly mentioned in the previous chapter, a number of Polish pilots who did not expect to see operational flying in France had volunteered for aircrew training in Britain soon after arriving in western Europe – the first of these pilots was absorbed into the RAF in January 1940. The air force had initially planned to use the Polish aircrewmen exclusively within newly-formed bomber units, and amongst those who accepted the conversion in a desperate bid to fly operationally once again were such aces as Skalski and Urbanowicz!

Subjected to training in all aspects of RAF procedure and regulations, the ex-PAF men found that the lack of a common language significantly affected their progress, for few spoke any English. This problem had not been encountered in France for the Poles had enjoyed a special relationship with this nation for many years, resulting in most pilots learning French – they also spoke German or Russian (the enemys' languages).

After France fell Britain was left alone in the fight against the Germans. Once the initial language problems had been solved, the first English-speaking Polish fighter pilots were posted to RAF squadrons in July 1940, where they soon flew operational sorties. Most of the remaining ex-PAF pilots promptly learned English procedures, and once in the frontline, their experience and fighting tactics was found to be surprisingly good.

The first aerial victory claimed by a Polish pilot in the RAF was achieved on 19 July 1940 when Flg Off Ostowicz of No 145 Sqn shared in the destruction of a He 111 with Plt Off M Newling – sadly, Ostowicz would also later become the first Polish pilot killed during the Battle of Britain (on 11 August). A fellow Pole within No 145 Sqn subsequently became the 'ace of aces' – Plt Off Witold Urbanowicz. He had opened his score with No 601 Sqn on 8 August when he downed a Bf 109 of I./JG 27, and after following up this success with another kill whilst part of No 145 Sqn, he was posted to No 303 (Polish) Sqn, where he would become the unit's top PAF ace.

Before Polish units were formed and trained within the RAF, nearly 100 Polish pilots had reinforced established fighter squadrons (including Blenheim nightfighting units). Poles would frequently move

Plt Offs Urbanowicz, Witorzeńć and Ostoja-Ostaszewski are seen at the PAF Depot at Blackpool awaiting their respective postings to RAF squadrons in mid-1940. During the Battle of Britain they would score a combined total of more than 20 confirmed kills. Note that in the early summer of 1940, Poles wore the standard RAF uniform adorned with shoulder flashes bearing the word 'POLAND' and a PAF eagle on the left breast pocket. Later, the traditional Polish *gapa* (pilot's wings) would replace its RAF equivalent, whilst the eagle would move from the tunic to the cap – as had previously been the case in Poland

Probably the most famous Polish pilot flying with British-manned units in 1940 was Sgt Antoni Głowacki of No 501 Sqn, who became 'an ace in a day' when he was credited with five kills on 28 August. Here is seen here next to his favourite Hurricane (V7234) giving the squadron Intelligence Officer a verbal report just minutes after landing

from one unit to another, and many fought with two or more RAF squadrons. During the Battle of Britain they flew operationally with Nos 17, 23, 32, 43, 54, 56, 65, 74, 85, 111, 145, 151, 152, 213, 229, 234, 238, 249, 253, 257, 501, 601, 603, 605, 607, 609 and 615 Sqns.

Looking at specific units, No 501 Sqn boasted three Polish aces during the summer of 1940, namely Plt Off Witorzeńć (who scored four and one shared kills), Plt Off Skalski (who also got four) and Sgt Głowacki. The latter became 'an ace in a day' on 24 August when he downed three Bf 109s and two Ju 88s in three sorties – all in lucky Hurricane I V7234. He added another Bf 109 four days later, and finished the month with a tally of eight kills and three damaged. On 18 September he was shot down, and after recovering from his injuries, was posted to No 611 Sqn.

In early August Biggin Hill-based No 32 Sqn welcomed three Polish pilots – Jan Pfeiffer, Karol Pniak and Bolesław Własnowolski, who were known to their English friends as 'Fife', 'Cognac' and 'Vodka' respectively. Pniak 'made ace' two weeks after his arrival, adding three kills to his 1939 score. However, Własnowolski (with a shared kill from Poland) was not expected to become achieve such status for his first flight under the watchful eye of Plt Off J L 'Polly' Flinders ended in a garden just outside the airfield! His first combat sortie on 14 August also saw him having to force-land his Hurricane (V7223) – this time near Dover. The following day, however, he downed his first 'Hun' over Britain;

'I flew as No 3 in "Red" section, when I spotted 9 Me 109s above me in V formation. I climbed and attacked one Me 109 from behind. We started to circle, when the Me 109 dived. I sent him a good burst and the Me 109 started to burn, and was diving towards the sea. I turned back towards the other Me 109s but was unable to catch up with any. Glycol temperature in my aeroplane was so high that I landed in a field in Essex. The aeroplane is temporarily unserviceable as the undercarriage was torn off landing on soft terrain.'

On 18 August Własnowolski claimed a Dornier, whilst later that afternoon – over Canterbury – he and Flt Lt Peter Malan Brothers shared in the destruction of a 7./JG 26 Bf 109E-1 flown by Lt Müller-Duhe. The Pole used only 600 rounds in four short bursts to down the enemy air-

Among the Battle of Britain aces who had seen combat over Poland in September 1939, Flg Off Tadeusz Nowierski was an outsider, for he had flown PZL.23 Karaś reconnaissance bombers during the campaign. It was not until he joined No 609 Sqn that he had a chance to fly a fighter in combat, although his lack of previous experience in this type of aircraft seemed not to hinder him too much – Nowierski emerged from the Battle of Britain as a fully fledged ace, being credited with five German aircraft destroyed, and having been awarded a DFC! The latter was presented to Nowierski by AVM Sir Quintin Brand, OC No 10 Group, on 10 June 1941, by which time the Polish ace was flying Hurricanes with No 316 Sqn

Battle of Britain ace Józef Jeka is seen posing for the camera (standing in the middle) whilst serving as a flying instructor at No 8 SFTS in Montrose, Scotland, in 1941. The student pilot seated immediately above him (middle) is Władysław Potocki, who would attain ace status by war's end. The latter individual went on to become a test pilot after the cessation of hostilities, being the first Pole to fly at Mach 2. Jeka also enjoyed a colourful career postwar, involving himself in clandestine missions with the Americans until he was apparently killed in a Lockheed U-2 crash (*Tilston via Drecki*)

craft. On 13 September Własnowolski moved to No 607 Sqn at Tangmere, and two days later he shot a Do 17Z down into the sea. On 17 September he was posted to No 213 Sqn (which was also based at Tangmere), where he claimed his last victory on 15 October. Własnowolski was killed on 1 November – the day he received a posting to a Polish fighter squadron – when he was shot down in Hurricane I N2608/AK-V soon after scrambling in response to a surprise low level attack on the airfield.

Despite these successes, language problems continued to arise throughout 1940, particularly within 'mixed' units like No 238 Sqn, as the following extract from the unit's Operations Record Book (Form 541) details – 'Slight difficulty in air-to-air communications, as Yellow 2 is a Polish pilot'. These problems sometimes resulted in confusing, or dangerous, situations arising in combat, but they did not impede No 238 Sqn's Sgt Jeka scoring four and one shared kills and two damaged.

Photographed in 1941 alongside his personal Hurricane II (Z2773/WX-T), Flt Lt Czerwiński was one of the most successful Polish pilots of the Battle of France. He added a German bomber to his tally in September 1940 whilst flying Hurricane I V6571/WX-Q, and subsequently achieved further victories in 1941. After experiencing innumerable combats, Czerwiński was finally killed in 1942 whilst serving as OC No 306 Sqn

Language problems affected both sides. As some Polish names were rather difficult for British personnel to pronounce, nicknames came in handy. For example, No 74 Sqn's highly successful 'Polish pair', Plt Offs Szczęsny and Brzezina, became 'Sneezy' and 'Breezy' respectively, whilst Plt Off Ostoja-Ostaszewski and Flg Off Nowierski of No 609 Sqn were known as 'Osti' and 'Novi'. When the latter two arrived at the unit in early August 'neither could speak much English, but both rapidly acquired efficiency on Spitfires', according to No 609 Sqn's Form ORB.

No 303 Sqn pilots relax at their dispersal at Northolt in September 1940. They are , from left to right, Sgt Karubin (6 confirmed victories during the Battle of Britain), Flg Off Januszewicz (note that he is still wearing his French uniform!), Plt Off Ferić (7 kills in the Battle), unknown and Sgt Szaposznikow (8 kills during the summer of 1940)

This same source also gives an interesting account of the action of 28 November when German ace Major Helmut Wick of JG 2 was shot down. Historians tend to accept that he fell victim to Flt Lt John Dundas of No 609 Sqn, who was in turn killed by Wick's wingman just minutes later. However, the No 609 Sqn ORB states;

'No 152 Sqn was also engaged at the same time and place, and it is considered possible that either one of their pilots, Sgt Klein (Poland) or Dundas, may have been responsible for bringing down the German Ace – Major Wick.'

Sgt Zygmunt Klein had one shared kill from 1939, to which he had added two confirmed destroyed, a probable and a damaged with the RAF before the 28 November mission from which he too failed to return.

Polish Squadrons

No 302 Sqn was the first Polish fighter unit to enter the battle, being formed at Leconfield in August 1940 with a British squadron leader at its helm, supported by two British flight commanders. Aside from its number, the unit also adopted the name 'City of Poznań' so as to allow it to inherit the traditions of the PAF's Poznań-based fighter *Eskadras*. Comprised mainly of ex-GC I/145 pilots, No 302 Sqn boasted French campaign aces Główczyński and Nowakiewicz within its ranks of seasoned combat veterans. Despite having such talented pilots, the unit produced just one ace during the Battle of Britain (Plt Off Chałupa), for No 302 Sqn primarily operated north of the main fighting area with No 12 Group. Chałupa claimed the first combat victory (a probable Ju 88) scored by a Polish pilot in a Polish squadron on 24 August. He then distinguished himself on No 302 Sqn's 'big day' – 15 September 1940 – when his unit claimed six Do 17s destroyed and four probables (includ-

Marian Pisarek was one of the most successful Polish fighter pilots of World War 2, his first kills (two and one shared victories) being achieved in September 1939 whilst serving as *141 Eskadra*'s deputy commander. Having fled Poland, he then flew with No 303 Sqn during the Battle of Britain (when this photograph was taken), claiming four kills and a damaged. Between July and October 1941, whilst flying Spitfires with No 308 Sqn, Pisarek added a further five and one shared kills, plus a probable. Appointed OC Northolt Wing on 19 April 1942, he was shot down and killed ten days later by JG 26 *Experte* Joachim Müncheberg (*Kopański*)

ing a fighter) at midday. Chałupa destroyed his fifth aircraft during this action. That afternoon No 302 Sqn scored two more kills, one of which fell to distinguished unit pilot Flg Off 'Roch' Kowalski.

The squadron flew Hurricanes until late 1941, Battle of France heroes Sqn Ldr Mümler, Flg Off Czerwiński, Plt Off Król and Sgt Nowakiewicz, as well as Plt Off Sporny and Sqn Ldr Witorzeńć, all scoring kills on type.

The second Polish fighter unit to form was No 303 Sqn, which was named 'City of Warsaw' because the majority of its personnel came from *111* and *112 Eskadras*. Most of its pilots were combat veterans, having flown in both Poland and France. They started conversion training on Masters on 2 August 1940, and received Hurricanes a few days later. Although it was the second Polish unit to enter combat, No 303 Sqn would subsequently become the most famous PAF squadron of them all.

The unit's first taste of combat came on 30 August 1940 when, during a routine training flight led by Sqn Ldr Kellett, German bombers were spotted being attacked by Hurricanes of No 213 Sqn north of Northolt.

No 303 Sqn's Hurricane I P3700/RF-E was flown by no less than four of the unit's aces in 1940 – Flg Offs Ferić, Zumbach and Henneberg and Sgt Wünsche. *Feric* used it to shoot down a Bf 109 over Sevenoaks on 6 September 1940, but the Hurricane was in turn lost just three days later when Sgt Wünsche was forced to take to his 'chute after being badly shot up. Note the unit badge under the windscreen rather than behind the cockpit. On the topic of unit markings, No 303 Sqn *did not* apply the Polish square to their aircraft, the only Hurricanes so adorned at Northolt being fighters that had been transferred in from No 302 Sqn as attrition replacements (*Koniarek*)

Sgt Eugeniusz Szaposznikow's lucky Hurricane V7244/RF-C is seen undergoing maintenance in late August 1940. Although he used V7242/RF-B to shoot down his first Bf 109 on 31 August 1940, his subsequent eight kills were all made in V7244. Prior to the Battle of Britain, 'Szaposzka' had flown MS.406s, MB.152s and D.520s in France as part of por. Arsen Cebrzyński's section within GC II/6. His first claim had been achieved on 15 June 1940 near Troyes when he shared in the destruction of a Hs 126 with Cebrzyński and kpr. Brzezowski (both future No 303 Sqn pilots). After the Battle of Britain, 'Szaposzka' flew with No 316 Sqn. He survived the war and settled in Britain, where he lived until his death in 1991

Plt Off Paszkiewicz saw the combat taking place 1000 ft below him, and decided to join in – he rapidly downed a 'Do 17' (probably a Bf 110).

No 303 Sqn would subsequently have many busy days at Northolt until being relieved on 7 October. One of the first combats (31 August) was described by future ace Sgt Wünsche;

'Flying as Yellow 2, I was protecting the Flight from behind, together with por. Ferić. Seeing the Huns attacking our Red section, I approached one of those who attacked Sgt Karubin. Of course my aim was to scare the enemy, or divert his attention. However, he then made a rapid manoeuvre, showing his crosses which made me even more angry. Suddenly one of the Me 109s jumped in front of me, below to the left. Without thinking I pushed the trigger button, and I spotted smoke. To be more sure I fired another burst, after which the burning Me dived to the ground. I made a few circles at the site of the encounter, looking for the others, but in vain, as they were busy finishing off their Huns.'

Nearly six weeks of hard fighting resulted in No 303 Sqn achieving the top score for any RAF fighter unit of the Battle of Britain - 126 confirmed kills - despite the squadron having only participated in the second half of the campaign! Urbanowicz, Karubin, Henneberg, Zumbach, Szaposznikow, Ferić, Paszkiewicz, Łokuciewski and Pisarek all achieved five or more kills, although nine pilots had also been killed – including aces Plt Off Paszkiewicz and Sgt Josef Frantisek (a Czech). The unit's pilots became war heroes back in Poland, with 'pirate' copies of the book *303 Squadron* being read by many young people in the occupied homeland.

On 11 October 1940 the exhausted No 303 Sqn moved to Leconfield. There, it filled the role of an intensive fighter training unit, with its many veteran pilots serving as instructors. In early 1941 it re-equipped with Spitfires and returned to Northolt, but that is quite another story . . .

Hurricane I P3120/RF-A was flown by several aces of No 303 Sqn during the Battle of Britain, including Flt Lt Urbanowicz and Flg Off Henneberg. The purpose of the diagonal stripe just forward of the tail surfaces remains a mystery, with a similar marking being applied to at least one other squadron Hurricane – it could have been a rank emblem, similar to those applied to P.11 fighters (see profile 2 for a comparison). This Hurricane had been transferred in from No 302 Sqn, so it almost certainly had the Polish square painted beneath the cockpit (see profile 13)

PAF REBORN

'I had been a little doubtful of the effect which their experience in their own countries and in France might have had upon the Polish and Czech pilots, but my doubts were laid to rest, because their squadrons swung into the fight with a dash and enthusiasm which is beyond praise. The first Polish squadron (No 303) in No 11 Group, during the course of one month, shot down more Germans than any British unit in the same period. Used in small numbers in British squadrons they fought very gallantly, but the language was a difficulty, and they were probably most efficiently employed in their own national units' – an extract from a report written by ACM Dowding for the Air Council.

Grp Cpt Pawlikowski (right) and Wg Cdrs Urbanowicz (centre) and Janus (left) enjoy a friendly chat between sorties. Pawlikowski, a veteran of the 1920 Polish-Bolshevik war and a famous pilot in the inter-war period, was made the Polish Liaison Officer to HQ Fighter Command, RAF, (i.e. commander of the Polish fighter units) following the formation of the PAF. Every now and then he would participate in offensive operations in order to remain familiar with frontline flying, but this practice came to an abrupt halt on 15 May 1943 when he failed to return from a mission over France. Another 'Circus', 'Rodeo' and 'Ramrod' veteran, Wg Cdr Janus had scored six kills by the time he was forced to bale out of his Spitfire over France in January 1943. He spent the rest of the war as a PoW (*Wandzilak*)

In the wake of such success, it was now obvious that more Polish squadrons should be formed as quickly as possible. PAF expansion was also encouraged by Gen Władysław Sikorski, Polish Commander-in-Chief. He had understood for some time that the only way to take the fight directly to the Germans was from the air, and he wanted strong Polish representation in any such force.

By war's end the PAF in exile would consist of 14 squadrons, including nine fighter units. This sizeable force was fully integrated into the RAF structure, just like the squadrons of other occupied countries. Płk Stefan Pawlikowski, commander of *Brygada Pościgowa* in 1939, was appointed as the first commander of the Polish fighter force, his official title being Polish Liaison Officer to HQ Fighter Command. Despite recognition by the RAF of the newly-reformed

Flt Lt Kazimierz Bronisław Kosiński had opened his score with three shared kills and two shared damaged during the fighting in France in June 1940. He then added two confirmed and two probable victories whilst serving as a flight commander with the Spitfire-equipped No 72 Sqn during 1941 (*Wandzilak*)

PAF, Pawlikowski and his staff had little independence in operational planning. Indeed, their primary role was to ensure that the postwar PAF had a skilled staff of commanders ready to control the frontline force. After Pawlikowski's death on operations in May 1943, his place was taken by płk Jerzy Bajan, who had been a distinguished pre-war fighter and aerobatic team leader.

Polish units were organised by reassembling personnel from pre-war units – *Eskadras* of *4 Pułk Lotniczy* reformed as No 306 'City of Toruń' Sqn, adopting its familiar duck emblem, whilst *2 Pułk Lotniczy*'s surviving personnel formed No 308 'City of Cracow' Sqn, adopting *121 Eskadra's* winged arrow badge. As more squadrons were created, so the number of pre-war regiments suitable for reassembly was exhausted. This resulted in new units simply adopting towns as their patron base and badge's from single *Eskadra*. For example, No 315 Sqn adopted Dęblin as it patron base (a city dear to every Polish pilot), while the unit's badge was modelled on that previously used by Warsaw-based *112 Eskadra*. No 316 Sqn had personnel from two other Warsaw *Eskadras* within *1 Pułk Lotniczy* (Nos 113 and 114), so it became the second 'City of Warsaw' squadron. Despite sharing the same title as No 303 Sqn, the two units were rarely confused as the latter outfit was known as the 'Kościuszko' Squadron – the fame of the latter unit's name, and its recent Battle of Britain glory, were important factors in convincing many Polish Americans to join the Polish armed forces in exile during the later war years. The last day-fighter unit formed was No 317 Sqn, which was activated around a cadre of personnel from Wilno-based *5 Pułk Lotniczy* – hence its name 'City of Wilno'.

Jerzy Jankiewicz had flown with No 601 Sqn during the Battle of Britain prior to joining No 303 Sqn – he eventually assumed command of this unit in July 1941. Jankiewicz later became not only the first Polish pilot to become OC of a British-manned squadron, but also the first to lead a British-manned wing on operations

6 Pułk Lotniczy personnel formed No 307 'City of Lwów' Sqn, which was selected to become a nightfighter unit and was duly equipped with Defiants rather than the usual Hurricanes. This specialist role did not appeal to the majority of the squadron's pilots, however, who had little appetite for being simply nocturnal 'gunbus-drivers'. Although the unit initially experienced considerable personnel movement, gradually it attracted those pilots from other squadrons who enjoyed night flying.

To denote its role, No 307 Sqn adopted the nickname *Lwowskie Puchacze* ('Lwów Owls'), producing a distinctive nightflyers' emblem which consisted of an owl clawing an aeroplane under a crescent moon. Although the only *dedicated* Polish nightfighter unit, No 307 Sqn was not the only Polish fighter unit flying at night. Indeed, credit for the second Polish nocturnal kill went to No 306 Sqn, whose Flg Off Władysław Nowak destroyed a He 111 whilst flying a Hurricane II at 0115 hours on 11 May 1941. That same night squadronmate Flg Off Gerard Ranoszek damaged a second bomber – Ranoszek subsequently found nightfighting so attractive that he transferred to No 307 Sqn and later became its CO. He finished the war as the second top-scoring Polish nightfighter pilot.

The last Polish squadron assigned fighters would not receive such aircraft until late 1944, No 309 'Ziemia Czerwieńska' Sqn initially being formed in 1941 as a Lysander-equipped army co-operation unit (hence its

Spitfire Mk VB AD233 was used by ace Sqn Ldr Milne during his time as OC No 222 Sqn, and when Jankiewicz took over the unit, he also inherited the aircraft. On 25 May 1942 Sqn Ldr Jerzy Jankiewicz was killed whilst flying this aeroplane during 'Rodeo 51' over Gravelines (*Arnold*)

Right
Presentation Spitfire VB AD257 'Borough of Willesden' was coded WX-A whilst with No 302 Sqn. Ace Flg Off Główczyński used the fighter on 30 December 1941 to destroy a Bf 109F (*Główczyński*)

No 303 Sqn was the first Polish unit to receive Spitfires, re-equipping with Mk Is in early 1941. 'Kościuszko' squadron veteran Maj Merian Cooper visited the unit at around the same time as the first Spitfires arrived at Northolt, and he is seen here with Plt Offs Ferić and Zumbach. Note that the traditional badge was still applied behind the cockpit on the Spitfire I, just as it had been with the Hurricane (*Koniarek*)

Bird Strike! Hiding behind a flock of seagulls is Spitfire V AD140/JH-H, which was delivered to No 317 Sqn in mid-October 1941 as one of the first Mk Vs issued to the PAF. A closer examination of this unusual photograph reveals that the aircraft's propeller hub is heavily soiled with oil that has leaked from the pitch control mechanism – a common Spitfire fault at that time! Other unclear contemporary black-and-white photographs of No 317 Sqn's aircraft also suffering with pitch control mechanism leaks gave rise to the legend of the unit's aircraft having their spinners painted red-and-white! In fact Polish colours were only applied in standard form, with a regulation PAF square on the aircraft's nose and the word 'POLAND' stencilled immediately beneath it. Finally, the No 317 Sqn badge was painted on behind the cockpit. Aside from being flown by No 317 Sqn pilots, AD140 was also used by ace Wg Cdr Witorzeńć, OC Exeter Wing, in early 1942 (*Bochniak*)

name, for non-fighter squadrons were christened after provinces). The myriad role changes that this outfit experienced directly reflected the RAF's various changes of heart in respect to how best the army co-operation role could be fulfilled. Having shown its obsolescence in France in 1940, the Lysander's period of tenure with No 309 Sqn was always going to be short, and the unit was duly selected to become the first RAF squadron to re-equip with the ultimately disastrous, US Navy inspired, Brewster Bermuda dive-bomber in early 1942. Following the latter project's abject failure, Douglas Boston light bombers were in turn proposed.

Eventually, however, the unit converted to Mustang Is, and successfully undertook the tactical recce role. In 1944 it was decided that the PAF had to make do with just one recce unit, and Italy-based No 318 Sqn was duly selected. No 309 Sqn was instructed to replace it Mustang Is with Merlin-powered Mustang IIIs, moving to Fighter Command in the process. The Mustang swap was thought to be the most sensible move by senior RAF officers, who assumed that the differences between the two types would be minimal – at least in respect to their flying characteristics. This may have indeed been the case, but when it came to 'fighting' in the Mustang III, No 309 Sqn's pilot had no experience of air combat. Therefore, the unit initially re-equipped with Hurricane IIs purely for tuitional purposes, which were in turn replaced by Mustang Is so as to allow the Poles to familiarise themselves with the American fighter once again! Finally, in late December 1944 No 309 Sqn was declared operational.

As the number of units grew, so old 'local rivalries' were revived in numerous forms. Squadron personnel did their best to stand apart from other outfits, and aside from unit badges (applied to both aircraft and uniforms), other 'quick recognition markings' were introduced. For example, all flying personnel would wear scarves in colours denoting their respective units – light brown for No 302, scarlet for No 303, green for No 306, white for No 308, blue for No 315, dark red for No 316 and light blue for No 317. Easily the most flamboyant PAF scarves were those worn by the nightfighting crews of No 307 Sqn, the turquoise neck-wear being adorned with a modified unit badge which had the aeroplane motif replaced by a bottle. Finally, when No 309 Sqn moved to Fighter Command, its pilots donned white-dotted navy blue scarves.

Flg Off Stabrowski's Spitfire VB of No 308 Sqn undergoes maintenance at Northolt sometime in the summer/autumn of 1941 – note that his 'Drunken Angel' personal emblem is being pointed out to the photographer by the rigger seated on the edge of the Spitfire's cockpit. No 308 Sqn was the most successful Polish fighter unit of 1941, being credited with 52 confirmed kills, 10 probables and 13 damaged during the course of the year (*Wandzilak*)

On completion of his tour, Flg Off Główczyński (middle) was invited to become an adjutant to Gen Władysław Sikorski (left), the Commander-in-Chief of the Polish Armed Forces. The PAF owed much to Sikorski, who insisted on expanding the service even if it meant drawing personnel away from ground and naval units (*Główczyński via Wojciech Łuczak*)

Unit identity could also be denoted by the way in which the Polish red-and-white national marking was applied to aircraft. No 303 Sqn exhibited the most prominent difference here by simply not carrying the marking until early 1942 – the famous 'Kościuszko' badge was considered to be Polish enough! No 302 Sqn, on the other hand, preferred to apply the national marking rather than the unit badge, the former usually being painted under the cockpit of squadron aircraft until mid-1942. Finally, No 306 Sqn applied the PAF square to the rear fuselage of its Spitfires again until 1942.

No 308 Sqn was the first unit to put the national marking on the cowling of its aircraft, thus allowing the red-and-white square to be applied in considerably larger dimensions. Subsequently, Nos 315, 316 and 317 Sqns followed suit, albeit with a reduced size national marking. Within two years, RAF regulations had been formulated which stipulated that

No 315 Sqn Spitfire VBs escort Gen Kazimierz Sosnkowski during his flight back to London from the unit's base at Ballyhalbert, near Belfast. This photo was taken in August 1943 by Flg Off Główczyński, who remained an adjutant to new Polish C-in-C, Gen Sosnkowski, following his appointment to the post in the wake of Gen Sikorski's death. The second of the two Mk Vs is BL993 PK-X, which is being flown here by Flg Off Edward Jaworski. Note that both aircraft lack unit badges, whilst BM537 is also devoid of a PAF marking. By this stage of the war the Spitfire V was past its best as a fighter, these worn-out aircraft being used primarily for training purposes at remote bases, where they were handed from one unit to another as squadrons rotated back and forth between the frontline and Northern Ireland. The small protrusion behind the tailwheel of both aircraft is a target-towing attachment (*Główczyński*)

the PAF marking could only be applied on the nose cowling under the exhaust stubs. The size of the marking was also standardised at 6 x 6 in following Air Ministry Order A926 (issued on 12 December 1940), which stated that 6 x 9 in had been allocated for the national insignia. The word 'POLAND' was therefore often added above or below the square to make full use of the permitted space.

Although most Polish fighter pilots had been gathered in PAF units by the spring of 1941, some continued to fly with RAF squadrons – with several attaining flight or squadron commander rank. Sqn Ldr Jerzy Jankiewicz became the first Pole to command a British-manned unit when he was appointed OC No 222 'Natal' Sqn in May 1942.

Twelve months earlier, Polish pilots Flt Lt Kosiński (of No 72 Sqn) and Sgt Pietrasiak of (No 92 Sqn) had become aces whilst flying with RAF units during the summer of 1941. Later in the war, ace Plt Off Blok also enjoyed success whilst flying with an RAF squadron when he shared a damaged claim against a Ju 88 on 31 May 1942. This may not seem like an important score for an ace on first examination, but it was in fact the premier success for the recently-formed No 164 'Times of Ceylon' Sqn. Based at Skeabrae, and equipped with Spitfire Mk Vs, the unit was tasked with providing the air defence for the naval base at Scapa Flow. Conditions at this northern airfield were often far from comfortable, and a posting to '164' was often considered to be the ideal way to cool down overheating tempers (this was certainly the case with Blok) by Fighter Command's 'senior brass'. Several other Polish pilots were also posted to the unit during its time in the Orkneys, with Flt Lt Ignacy Olszewski actually serving as 'A' Flight commander for some months.

No Polish pilots achieved ace status as nightfighers during the war, the highest scorer being Sgt Michał Turzański with four bombers confirmed destroyed whilst flying Beaufighters with No 307 Sqn during 1941/42. This photograph was taken on 2 November 1941 after he had claimed a pair of II./KG 2 Dornier bombers shot down the previous night (*Bochniak*)

111 Eskadra

112 Eskadra

113 Eskadra

114 Eskadra

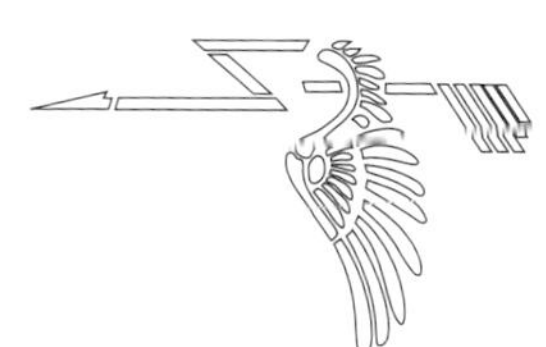
121 Eskadra

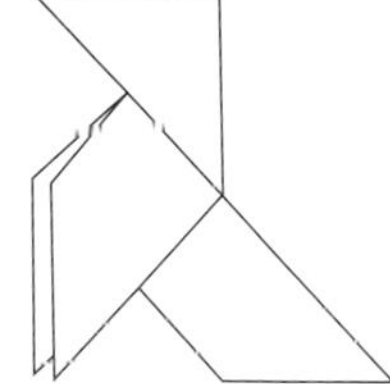
122 Eskadra

123 Eskadra

131 Eskadra

132 Eskadra

141 Eskadra

142 Eskadra

151 Eskadra

152 Eskadra

161 Eskadra

162 Eskadra

No 302 Sqn

No 303 Sqn

No 306 Sqn

No 308 Sqn

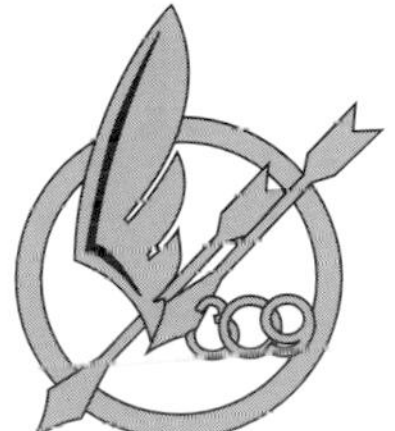
No 309 Sqn

No 315 Sqn

316 Sqn

No 317 Sqn

Colour Plates

1
P.11c 8.70 'White 10' of ppor. Hieronim Dudwał, *113 Eskadra*, Poniatów, September 1939

2
P.11c 8.110 'White 4' of kpr. Stanisław Brzeski, *152 Eskadra*, Szpandowo, September 1939

3
P.11c 8.63 'White 2' of ppor. Waclaw Król, *121 Eskadra*, Podlodów, September 1939

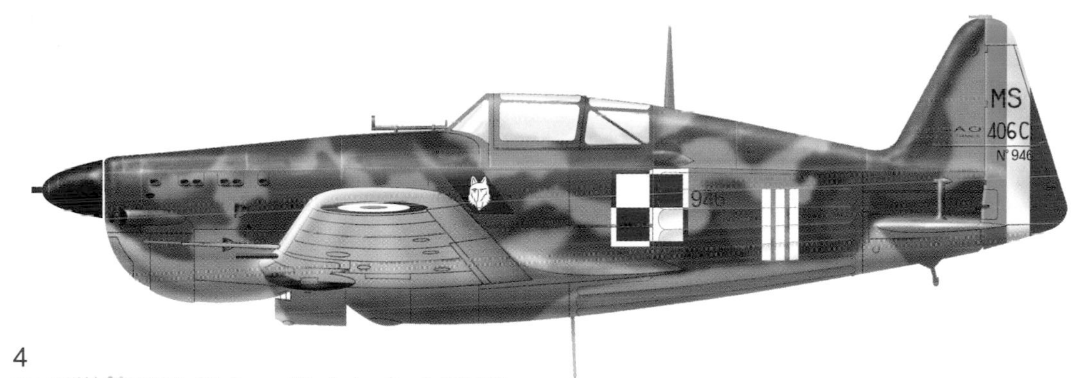

4
MS.406C1 936 'White III' of ppor. Władysław Gnyś, GC III/1, Moerbecke, May 1940

5
CR.714 Cyclone I-234 'White 2' of ppor. Czesław Główczyński, GC I/145, Villacoublay, May 1940

6
D.520C1 119 of ppłk Mieczysław Mümler, GC II/7, Luxeuil, June 1940

7
MB.151C1 57 of por. Zdzisław Henneberg, *Escadrille de Chasse et de Defence He*, Chateauroux, June 1940

8

Hurricane I P3208 of Sgt Antoni Głowacki, No 501 Sqn, Gravesend, August 1940

9

Hurricane I V7235 of Flg Off Ludwik Paszkiewicz, No 303 Sqn, Northolt, August 1940

10

Hurricane I V6605 of Plt Off Zdzisław Henneberg, No 303 Sqn, Northolt, 7 September 1940

11

Hurricane I P3939 of Sqn Ldr Witold Urbanowicz, OC No 303 Sqn, Northolt, September 1940

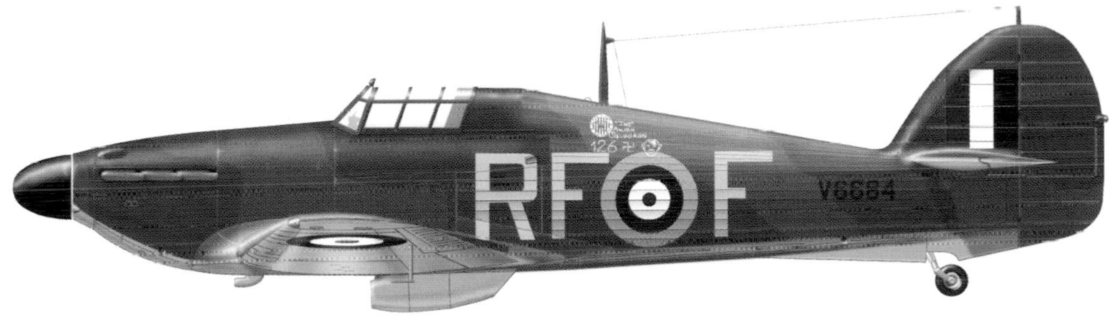

12
Hurricane I V6684 of Sqn Ldr Witold Urbanowicz, OC No 303 Sqn, Northolt, September 1940

13
Hurricane I V7504 of Sgt Stanisław Karubin, No 303 Sqn, Northolt, September 1940

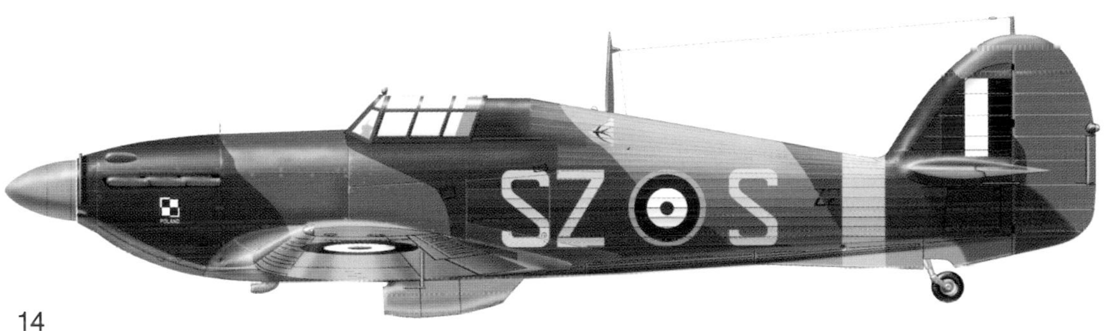

14
Hurricane II Z2405 of Flt Lt Aleksander Gabszewicz, No 316 Sqn, Church Stanton, summer 1941

15
Hurricane II Z3675 of Plt Off Kazimierz Sporny, No 302 Sqn, Church Stanton, September 1941

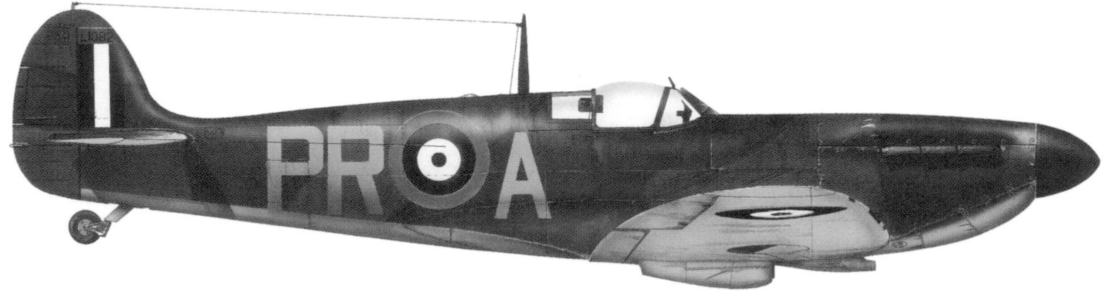

16

Spitfire I L1082 of Flg Off Tadeusz 'Novi' Nowierski, No 609 Sqn, Warmwell, 13 August 1940

17

Spitfire II P8079 of Flt Lt Wacław Łapkowski, No 303 Sqn, Northolt, March 1941

18

Spitfire II P8385 *IMPREGNABLE* of Flg Off Mirosław 'Ox' Ferić, No 303 Sqn, Northolt, May-July 1941

19

Spitfire II P7855 *KRYSIA* of Flg Off Jan 'Kon' Falkowski, No 315 Sqn, Northolt, July/August 1941

20

Spitfire II P8387 *HALINA/BARTY* of Sgt Stanisław 'Charlie' Blok, No 315 Sqn, Northolt, August 1941

21

Spitfire V AB824 of Sgt Marian Bełc, No 303 Sqn, Northolt, October 1941

22

Spitfire V W3506/RF-U *HENDON LAMB* of Sgt Mieczysław Adamek, No 303 Sqn, Northolt, December 1941

23

Spitfire V P8742 *Ada* of Flg Off Czesław Główczyński, No 302 Sqn, Harrowbeer, December 1941

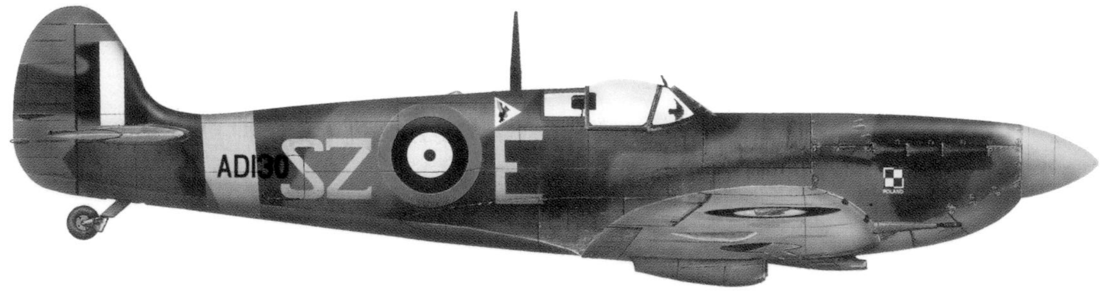

24

Spitfire V AD130 of Sqn Ldr Aleksander Gabszewicz, OC No 316 Sqn, Northolt, February 1942

25

Spitfire V W3970 of Flg Off Tadeusz Koc, No 317 Sqn, Exeter, early 1942

26

Spitfire V EN951/RF-D *Donald Duck* of Sqn Ldr Jan 'Johann' Zumbach, OC No 303 Sqn, Kirton-in-Lindsey, October/November 1942

27

Spitfire XII EN222 of Flt Lt Henryk Pietrzak and Flt Lt Władysław Potocki, Intensive Flying Development Flight, High Post, November 1942 to February 1943

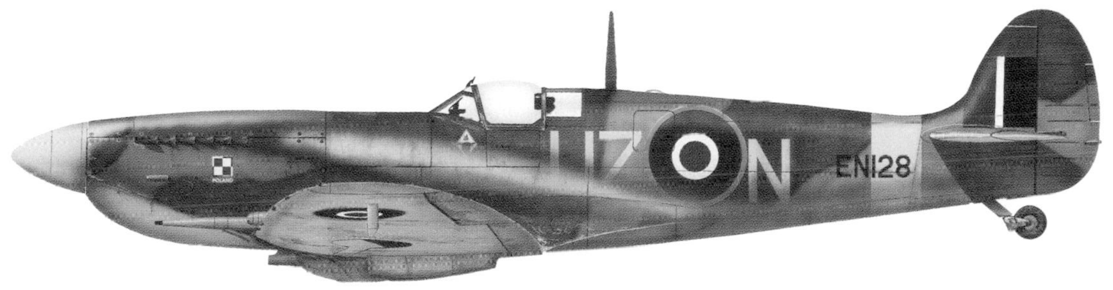

28

Spitfire IX EN128 of Flg Off Henryk Pietrzak, No 306 Sqn, Northolt, 31 December 1942

29

Spitfire V BM144 *Halszka* of Flg Off Antoni Głowacki, No 303 Sqn, Kirton-in-Lindsey, early 1943

30

Spitfire IX EN267 of Flt Sgt Kazimerz Sztramko, Polish Fighting Team, Goubrine, April 1943

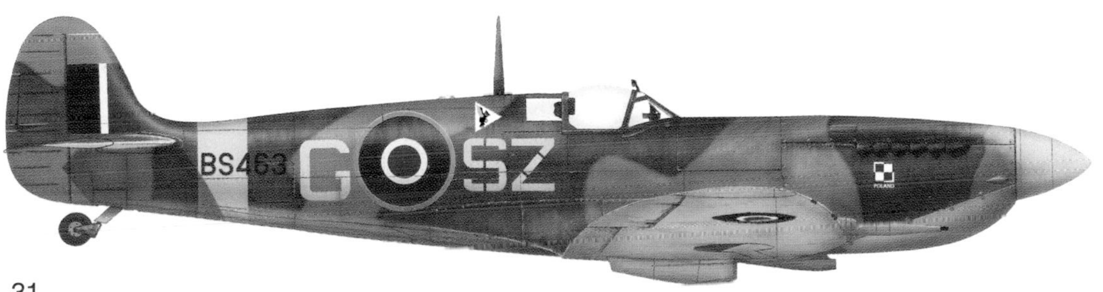

31

Spitfire IX BS463 of Flg Off Michal Miroslaw 'Miki' Maciejowski, No 316 Sqn, Northolt, May 1943

32

Spitfire IX EN172 of Flg Off Stanisław 'Charlie' Blok, No 315 Sqn, Northolt, May 1943

33

Spitfire IX LZ989 of Flt Lt Józef Jeka, No 316 Sqn, Northolt, August 1943

34

Spitfire VIII JF447 of Sqn Ldr Stanislaw 'Skal' Skalski, OC No 601 Sqn, Lentini West, August 1943

35

Spitfire IX MA259 of Sqn Ldr Eugeniusz 'Horby' Horbaczewski, OC No 43 Sqn, Cassala, 4 September 1943

36

Spitfire VC MA289 of Flt Lt Wladyslaw 'Maciek' Drecki, No 152 Sqn, Milazzo East, 11 September 1943

37

Spitfire IX MK370 of Wg Cdr Julian 'Roch' Kowalski, Wing Leader No 131 (Polish) Fighter Wing, Chailey, May 1944

38

Spitfire IX ML136 of Sqn Ldr Waclaw Król, OC No 302 Sqn, Ford, summer 1944

39

Spitfire XVI TD317 of Sqn Ldr Karol Pniak, OC No 308 Sqn, Nordhorn, April 1945

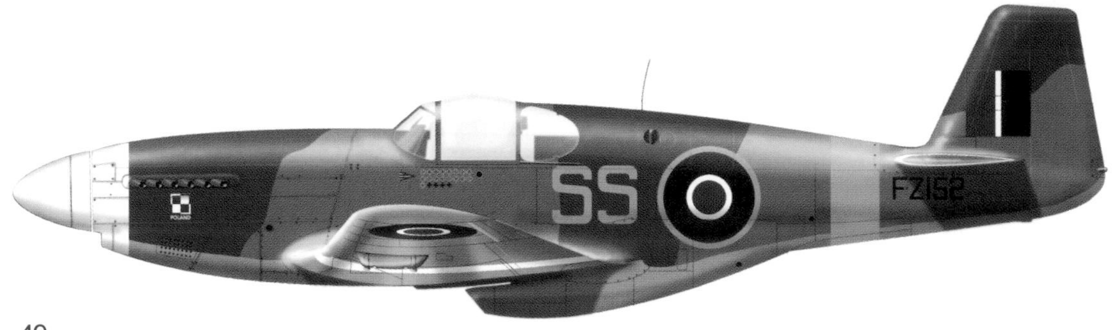

40
Mustang III FZ152 of Wg Cdr Stanisław Skalski, Wing Leader No 133 Wing, Coolham, May 1944

41
P-51B 43-6898 *The Deacon* of Maj Wacław (Winslow) 'Mike' Sobański, CO 334th FS/4th FG, Debden, May 1944

42
Mustang III FB145 of Flt Sgt Jakub Bargiełowski, No 315 Sqn, Coolham, May-June 1944

43
Mustang III FB166 of Sqn Ldr Eugeniusz 'Dziubek' Horbaczewski, OC No 315 Sqn, Brenzett, June 1944

44
Mustang III FZ196 of Flt Lt Władysław Potocki, No 306 Sqn, Coolham, June 1944

45
Mustang III HB886 of Grp Capt Tadeusz Nowierski, OC No 133 Wing, Brenzett, August 1944

46
Mustang III FB353 of Flt Lt Longin Majewski, No 316 Sqn, Friston, August 1944

47
Mustang III HB868 of Wg Cdr Jan 'Johann' Zumbach, Wing Leader No 133 Wing, Brenzett, September 1944

48

P-47D 42-25836 *PENGIE III* of Flt Lt Bolesław 'Mike' Gładych, 61st FS/56th FG, Boxted, May 1944

49

P-47D 42-26044 *Silver Lady* of Flt Lt Bolesław 'Mike' Gładych, 61st FS/56th FG, Boxted, July/August 1944

50

Mustang IVA KM112 of Sqn Ldr Bolesław 'Gandhi' Drobiński, OC No 303 Sqn, Coltishall, late 1945

51

Mustang IV KH663 of Wt Off Jakub Bargiełowski, No 303 Sqn, Hethel, 1946

1
Plut. Adolf Pietrasiak, *Escadrille Legere de Defence Ko*, Bourges, France, June 1940

2
Kpr. Jan Kremski of *121 Eskadra*, Balice, Poland, September 1939

3
Por. Wojciech Januszewicz, OC *111 Eskadra*, Młynów, Poland, September 1939

4

Sqn Ldr Henryk 'Hesio' Szczęsny, OC No 317 Sqn, Exeter, November 1941

5

Grp Capt Aleksander 'Hrabia Oleś' Gabszewicz, OC No 131 Wing, Vendeville, France, September 1944

6

Sgt Eugeniusz Nowakiewicz, No 302 Sqn, Heston, spring 1942

NORTHOLT WING

The association of RAF Northolt with the PAF commenced with No 303 Sqn's Battle of Britain exploits and would continue until D-Day. Throughout the war the Middlesex fighter station remained a frontline base, with its units being continuously employed in action over the continent. Therefore, the vast majority of the victories credited to Polish day fighter pilots over Europe in 1941-43 were scored by the Northolt Wing, which was referred to in Polish documentation as *1 Polskie Skrzydło Myśliwskie* (1st Polish Fighter Wing).

Although a further two Polish wings were subsequently formed at other airfields, it was Northolt that remained *the* Polish fighter base in Britain. Here, units would come and go, but they would always be manned by Poles. Indeed, the station was 'Polandized' to such extent that a sign reading 'English spoken' had to be erected in the Officers' Mess bar so as to reassure the occasional Allied guest confused by the language around him. Polish also became a principal tongue at the *Orchard* pub and dance-hall in nearby Ruislip, which was heavily frequented by Northolt personnel. Many a Polish airman also found an English bride whilst based there.

The wing was set up in 1941 under the joint command of John Kent and Witold Urbanowicz – neither man was a stranger to Northolt, for both had flown with No 303 Sqn during the Battle of Britain. The spring of 1941 saw RAF units mount their first offensive operations over the continent, and they were opposed by battle-proven *Jagdgeschwaderen*, based at Pas-de-Calais airfields, that were now operating over friendly territory, rather than over Britain. Air battles in French skies were as fierce as those seen during the summer of 1940, the air offensive across the Channel being intensified in the wake of the German invasion of the USSR.

The RAF would often undertake several missions a day, resulting in both growing victories, and losses, for Fighter Command. As an example of a typical day's flying, on 23 June 1941 the Northolt Wing flew two operations. During one of these sweeps, Battle of Britain veteran Sgt Wojciechowski scored his fifth kill, whilst later that same day future aces

Wg Cdr 'Johnny' Kent and his Battle of Britain companion Sqn Ldr Urbanowicz are seen whilst jointly commanding the newly-established Polish Wing at Northolt in 1941. Kent, who had previously served as 'A' Flight Commander with No 303 Sqn, held the Poles in high regard, as the following quote (written on the occasion of him leaving Northolt in late 1940 to take command of No 92 Sqn) from the squadron's chronicle clearly shows;

'It is with genuine regret and sorrow that I terminate my association with the squadron, the finest the RAF has seen. I can count the time I have spent with you as the most impressive and instructive of my life'

During the spring of 1941 No 303 Sqn re-equipped at Northolt with Spitfire IIs. P7962/RF-A *Inspiration* (its presentation name) was often flown during this period by Plt Off Gładych, who had yet to score his first of 17 victories. On 9 May this aeroplane was shot down by a III./JG 3 Bf 109, its pilot, Flg Off Zumbach, bailing out safely over Dover

Seriously damaged in combat during 'Circus 88' on 29 August 1941, Spitfire II P8342/UZ-N of No 306 Sqn was hastily landed at Biggin Hill on 29 August 1941 by its pilot, Sgt Marcin Machowiak. The Pole had claimed a Bf 109 during the mission, which had also seen four other Polish aces adding to their respective scores. P8342 bore the presentation name *CERAM* and a mysterious cartoon character which probably dated back to its service with No 145 Sqn. Note how No 306 Sqn has applied the squadron badge on the engine cowling and the Polish square on the rear fuselage (*Chołoniewski*)

Sgts Adamek and Wünsche also added to their scores. However, by far the most successful Pole on this date was Plt Off Gładych. At about midday, whilst No 303 Sqn was escorting 23 bombers from Redhill to Bethune ('Circus 19'), Gładych scored his very first kill. The same unit later sent 12 Spitfire IIs off again at 1935 to act as escorts for bombers flying between Dungeness and Le Touquet as part of 'Circus 20'. What follows is Gładych's report from that second mission (flown in P8330/RF-D), which saw him credited with two aircraft confirmed destroyed;

'I was flying in the first section of four of 303 Polish Sqn after an attack at Desvres aerodrome when I heard a warning on the R/T that Me 109s were about to attack us from astern. Looking behind me I spotted an Me 109 chasing a Spitfire and turned. I was able to engage the E/A and when it dived I followed, and on pulling out was dead astern of the German. At 50 yards I fired a short burst whereupon the E/A half-rolled and dived down in flames. I then found I was alone and although hearing my Squadron Leader instructing us to return home I could not see our aircraft. Approaching the coast I noticed 2 Me 109s 3000 ft above, one of which dived towards me. I swung away letting him pass me and then following him but after we had both pulled out and I was about to attack, the second E/A was on my tail. I turned and a dog-fight developed but another Me 109 joined in. I circled, at times going into tight turns and by this manner tried to reach the coast. I then observed 8-10 Me 109s circling above me which then took turns to dive at me, most of them firing. My engine was giving trouble and had probably been

No 308 Sqn commanders (left to right) Flt Lt Popławski, Sqn Ldr Żak, and Flt Lt Koc. Popławski scored his fifth kill in October 1941, while Koc 'made ace' in April 1942. Next to Koc is Plt Off Wandzilak who, on 21 September 1941 at 1512 hrs claimed a 'Bloch MB.151' destroyed. He had, in fact, become the first Polish pilot to be credited with the destruction of an Fw 190 (*Wandzilak*)

BL670/RF-K is seen at Northolt in early May 1942 whilst assigned to the newly-appointed Sqn Ldr Walerian Żak (centre, flanked by his flight commanders, Flt Lt Bieńkowski and Flt Lt Zumbach). Previously used by Sqn Ldr Kołaczkowski, BL670 still bore his nickname for the aircraft (*Krysia*), its presentation title *Ever Ready II* beneath the cockpit and the name *Wojtek* (pettified form of Wojciech) on the port-side engine cowling. This Spitfire was an ace in its own right, being credited with three and two shared kills to three different pilots (*Koniarek*)

hit and I could not turn easily. In addition I was beginning to feel very tired. Suddenly one E/A dived as though to attack an aircraft below me and I adopted the same tactics as before by following him down and pulling out behind him. My guns would however not fire. I had got quite close to the E/A by then, when he suddenly half rolled and my aircraft struck the Me 109, cutting off its tail unit. My cockpit cover was open and a piece of the E/A flew in and cut across my right eye. The stream of blood blinded me but I knew I was still over France at 14,000 ft. With an erratic engine I managed to cross the Channel and after informing Operations of my difficulties I intended to land at Manston. I was, however, practically unconscious by this time and cannot recollect anything further until I awoke in hospital'.

The following extract, taken from the Intelligence Officer's Report on Gładych's mission, describes the final moments of the flight which the pilot admitted to having no recollection of;

'P/O Gładych crash-landed in a field near Manston after his aircraft had hit a telegraph pole, the engine being torn from the aircraft which

Yet more senior pilots pose by another Northolt-based Spitfire V. Here, BM144/RF-D *Donald Duck* provides the backdrop for Flt Lts Zumbach (left), Bieńkowski (second from left) and Marciniak (third from left). This aircraft was Zumbach's mount during his time as No 303 Sqn's 'A' Flight Commander, and he used it to to claim an Fw 190 probable on 27 April 1942. He continued to fly BM144 after his appointment as OC of the unit on 25 May 1942. Note the tall rear-view mirror post fitted to this aircraft, which was a modification that Zumbach had carried out to all his Spitfires

AA853/WX-C of No 302 Sqn was photographed 'in the field' in early July 1942. The white stripes (note that they are also present across the upper surface of the tailplane as well) were applied during this month possibly as part of an Allied exercise. Despite extensive research, the authors have found no documentary proof that these markings were re-applied the following month for the Dieppe landings, as has often been claimed by historians

became a total wreck. The pilot has only recently been released from hospital, where he was treated for bad cuts on his face, a fractured skull and a fractured collar bone.'

The sheer intensity of operations during the summer of 1941 is graphically illustrated by the fact that barely two months later, on 29 August, 'Circus 88' was flown. Four Polish aces increased their scores on that day, three of whom were part of the Northolt Wing – Flt Lts Wesołowski and Janus of No 308 Sqn, and Sgt Chudek of No 315 Sqn. The Northolt Wing chronicle gave the following account of the mission;

'The "Wing" takes off at 0630 for "Circus 88" as "Escort Cover Wing". S/Ldr Rolski as leader in 306 Sqn. Altitudes: 306 – 18,000 ft, 308 – 19,000 and 315 – 21,000 ft. Rendezvous with bombers at Rye. Route Hardelot-Hazebrouck-Mardyck. French coast crossing at 0712. On the way formation shot at by the enemy at Hardelot, St Omer and Hazebrouck. Close to the target not far from Hazebrouck the Wing was attacked by Me 109s. Sgt. Machowiak from 306 chased one and after shooting it down was coming back to England at low altitude. During the

Taken possibly on the day of the Dieppe landings (19 August 1942), No 303 Sqn personnel are seen milling around listening to the sortie debriefing. On that day the unit was credited with seven and two shared German aircraft destroyed and a further four probably destroyed

flight he was attacked by 3 Me 109s. Having noticed bullet traces placed on his aeroplane, he hid in clouds, the base of which was 900 ft. In the middle of the Channel he left the clouds and on reaching England, due to lack of fuel landed at Biggin Hill at 0830. 2 hits of cannon shells were found in the tail controls, 8 holes in the port and 3 holes in starboard wing, as well as machine gun bullet hits on the armoured plate.

'From above Hazebrouck the Wing headed to Gravelines. Landing about 0820.

'**Enemy losses:**

1 Me 109 destroyed by	Sgt. Machowiak	of 306
2 Me 109 destroyed by	Sgt. Chudek	of 315
1 Me 109 damaged	ppor Woliński	of 315
1 Me 109 destroyed by	por. Wesołowski	of 308
1 Me 109 destroyed by	por. Janus	of 308
1 Me 109 destroyed by	Sgt. Zieliński	of 308

'**Own losses:**

306 Sqn	por. Słoński	missing
308 Sqn	ppor. Bettcher	missing
315 Sqn	por. Mickiewicz	missing (baled out)'

The same operation also saw Flt Lt Kosiński of No 72 Sqn (Biggin Hill Wing) credited with a Bf 109 confirmed and another probably destroyed.

Intensive operations continued until bad weather put a halt to these missions in November. No less than 16 Polish pilots had become aces

No 303 Sqn's AB174/RF-Q was used by Plt Off Antoni Głowacki to claim a share in a He 111 destroyed and an Fw 190 probably destroyed on 19 August 1942. The name bestowed upon this Spitfire had its roots in the language problems encountered by Poles in Britain. The Polish alphabet does not use the letter 'Q', which is therefore usually transcribed as 'KU', whilst the English sound for 'W' is best approximated by the Polish generic character of 'Ł'. The English pronunciation of 'C', like 'K', caused much confusion, too. Therefore, '*KUKUŁKA*' (Polish for cuckoo) became '*QQWCA*' when jokingly spelt 'the English way'! (*Koniarek*)

The Duke of Kent shakes hands with Sgt Kazmierz Sztramko whilst visiting No 317 Sqn at Northolt – Sztramko had flown with both *113 Eskadra* in 1939 and GC II/10 in France in 1940. At far left is Sqn Ldr Skalski, who was OC No 317 Sqn at that time, whilst in the middle of the photograph is Wg Cdr Janus, OC Northolt Wing. All three Polish pilots would achieve ace status by 1943 (*Bochniak*)

between May and December 1941, most of these men adding to their previous scores from Poland, France and the Battle of Britain. However, four Poles opened their scores during the summer of 1941, namely Drobiński, Chudek, Popławski and Janus. Plt Off Drobiński – known as 'Gandhi' due to his modest posture and firm character – was Poland's most successful Spitfire II ace with six kills during June-July 1941. On 21 June, while flying P8335/RF-R on 'Circus 16', he forced down no less a pilot than Oberstleutnant Adolf Galland (flying Stab./JG 26 Bf 109F-2 Wk-Nr 5776).

Compared with the hectic operations of the previous years, 1942 brought few additional victories for the Polish aces. The most successful day in a relatively barren year was 19 August, when the Northolt Wing flew in support of the disastrous Dieppe landings. No 303 Sqn was credited with seven and two shared kills, plus four probables, on this date, whilst No 317 Sqn also 'bagged' seven destroyed and one shared kill, plus a damaged, and the Northolt Wing HQ flight two damaged.

In November 1942 the PAF HQ announced that the combined score

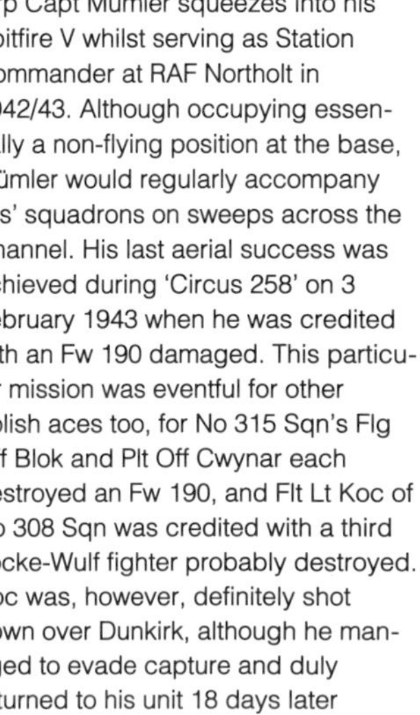

Grp Capt Mümler squeezes into his Spitfire V whilst serving as Station Commander at RAF Northolt in 1942/43. Although occupying essentially a non-flying position at the base, Mümler would regularly accompany 'his' squadrons on sweeps across the Channel. His last aerial success was achieved during 'Circus 258' on 3 February 1943 when he was credited with an Fw 190 damaged. This particular mission was eventful for other Polish aces too, for No 315 Sqn's Flg Off Blok and Plt Off Cwynar each destroyed an Fw 190, and Flt Lt Koc of No 308 Sqn was credited with a third Focke-Wulf fighter probably destroyed. Koc was, however, definitely shot down over Dunkirk, although he managed to evade capture and duly returned to his unit 18 days later

As mentioned in the previous caption, Flg Off Blok scored his third confirmed kill during 'Circus 258' whilst flying Spitfire IX BS409/PK-B. The future Polish ace did not have things all his own way, however, for his aircraft was so seriously damaged during the mission that Blok attempted to bale out. Only stopped by a jammed canopy, the pilot somehow managed to nurse his crippled Spitfire back home, where he later casually posed for this astonishing photograph (*Archiwum Dokumentacji Mechanicznej – Warszawa*)

Plt Offs Michał Cwynar (right) and Tadeusz Żurakowski pose by Spitfire IX BS513/PK-Z of No 315 Sqn. All of Cwynar's victories in Britain were scored with this unit, and he also became one of just three Polish fighter aces to achieved 'acedom' against the V1 – he was credited with one and four shared 'doodlebugs' during the summer of 1944 (*Cwynar*)

of all Polish fighter units flying in Britain had reached 499, and in order to mark the 500th kill, a prize of a silver shield was to be awarded. Bad weather prevented any encounters with the enemy for many weeks, but finally on 31 December 1942, Northolt Spitfire IXs managed to undertake 'Rodeo 140' over France. According to No 315 Sqn's ORB;

'10 miles N. of Abbeville, we were told by Ops that some of our squadrons were engaged over Berck by 20 FW 190s at 25,000. When we arrived on the scene, we saw only 6 FWs, and 306 Sqn, who were with us, received orders to attack, while we were to provide top cover. During this engagement, 306 Sqn downed 2 E/A, bringing the total destroyed by Polish pilots to 501. Unfortunately, they lost 2 pilots at the same time.'

As was all to often the case, victories and losses had come together, mixing joy with grief. The pilot credited with achieving the 500th PAF kill would subsequently achieve ace status. Plt Off Henryk Pietrzak excitedly claimed credit for the kill over the R/T well before he had landed back at

Northolt, whilst the 501st victory was awarded to Flg Off Zdzisław Langhamer. In the wake of the mission much publicity (and decorations) was lavished on both pilots, who met the Polish president and had their combat described by virtually every newspaper in Britain – whether published in Polish, English, French or Czech.

It should be remembered, however, that the PAF's 500 kills figure did not include victories claimed by Poles in British units. If these were counted, then the 500th kill would have officially come more than a year before, claimed by nightfighting (intruder) crew Flg Offs Reymer-Krzywicki (pilot), Strasburger (radio-navigator) and Bokowiec (air gunner), who flew with British-manned No 23 Sqn. On the night of 6 December 1941, whilst flying Havoc I BD112/YP-T, they were credited with their only successes of the war – a Ju 88 destroyed and another damaged.

Two aces of No 306 Sqn – Flt Sgt Pietrzak (seated on the wing) and Flg Off Sołogub. The latter pilot (along with 'Charlie' Blok) was a cadet officer at Dęblin when the war broke out, and he was hastily posted to a Polish squadron as an NCO – his commission, which was originally scheduled for 1940, eventually arrived once he was in England (*Arct*)

A group of No 316 Sqn pilots relax at dispersal in mid-1943. The Spitfire IX in the background (EN179/SZ-J *Jean*) was usually flown by Flt Lt Gnyś (seen here seated at far left with his back to the camera, talking to Flg Off Jerzy Szymankiewicz). EN170 was also flown on occasion by Flt Lt Maciejowski and Sgt Murkowski, the latter pilot using the aircraft to telling effect on 9 July 1943 when he was credited with an Fw 190 destroyed and a second probably destroyed (*Wagner*)

BS451/RF-M of No 303 Sqn was used by Flt Sgt Chudek to down two Fw 190s on 17 August 1943. According to the log-book of Sqn Ldr Falkowski, he also destroyed an Fw 190 with it on 6 September – interestingly, the unit's records state that Falkowski was flying MA524/RF-F on that particular mission! (*Choloniewski*)

SKALSKI'S CIRCUS

WITH TOMASZ DRECKI

During the later half of 1940, PAF pilots were credited with 214 enemy aircraft destroyed. The score for 1941 was 198, and in 1942 the figure had dropped to 90. Clearly, the Luftwaffe in Western Europe was no longer the powerful opponent it once was, meaning that PAF aces had fewer opportunities to add to their scores.

As the opposition weakened in Western Europe, so senior Allied strategists once again commenced planning for invasion. The success of such an undertaking would hinge on the control of the skies above the landing beaches, and dictate that fighter units operate closely with forces on the ground. In order to make themselves available over the battlefield at short notice, squadrons would have to become fully mobile, functioning effectively from temporary sites in-theatre well away from established bases.

This type of combat was not new to the fighter units of the Desert Air Force, and it was in order to gain valuable experience of just such operations in preparation for the D-Day invasion that plk Stefan Pawlikowski, Polish Liaison Officer to the RAF, requested that a group of experienced Polish fighter pilots be sent to the North African front.

The idea of operating in an exotic location where Axis aircraft appeared to be far more abundant attracted no less than 70 volunteers. Ultimately, just 15 pilots were selected, of which three were already aces – Stanisław Skalski (who would lead the unit in the air), Wacław Król and Karol Pniak. The latter pilot was one of the few Poles to have already encountered Italian aircraft in combat, scoring kills in November 1940 during the *Regia Aeronautica*'s fitful attacks on Britain. Król, meanwhile, had flown in Algerian and Tunisian skies in June 1940 with GC II/7.

The unit (known officially as the Polish Fighting Team – PFT) arrived in Africa in March 1943, where it was assigned to No 244 Wing (led by Wg Cdr Ian Gleed) and attached to No 145 Sqn (commanded by Sqn Ldr Lance Wade) for logistics purposes. The Poles soon got used to the high temperatures, harsh living conditions and flying activity comparable to that experienced during the Battle of Britain, pilots within the Desert Air Force also enjoying close comradeship – officers and NCOs lived, messed and entertained together.

Initially, the PFT was equipped with Spitfire Vs, which came as something of a disappointment for the pilots, who had been flying the vastly superior Mk IX back in Britain. However, after less than

'Skalski Circus' pilots (from left to right) Król, Majchrzyk, Popek, Drecki, Martel and Arct. This photo was taken after the combat on 20 April 1943 when all six pilots were credited with a kill apiece. Król was already an ace prior to him coming to Africa, and he added a further three kills to his tally during the Tunisian campaign. Popek, who had scored one and two shared kills with No 303 Sqn in Britain, added two more confirmed victories to his score whilst in Africa (*Arct*)

two weeks in-theatre, their request for better equipment was answered, and some of the first Spitfire IXs in Africa were allocated to the flight. Australian pilot W M Matheson, who was then with No 601 Sqn, recalls;

'When I joined the Wing in Tunisia, the Polish flight was the only one equipped with Spitfire Mk IXs – the rest flew Mk Vs, and the Poles usually flew top cover to various squadrons. I think they were officially known as the 'Polish Fighter Flight (Team)', but were occasionally referred to as "Skalski's Circus".'

Flying their new mounts, Skalski and Horbaczewski opened the scoring on 28 March 1943 when they each downed a Ju 88 – the latter pilot would score five kills whilst in Africa (adding to his previous score of three confirmed and one probably destroyed), thus becoming the only Polish 'ace of Africa'. Known for taking great risks in order to secure a kill, Horbaczewski enjoyed typically mixed results on 6 May when he attacked two Messerschmitts single-handedly whilst flying EN459/ZX-1.

'Dziubek' Horbaczewski poses with captured *Afrika Korps* equipment towards the end of the North African campaign (*Arct*)

Having quickly shot one of the fighters down, he was then hit by the remaining Bf 109. With his engine on fire, Horbaczewski intended to bale out, but his violent manoeuvring extinguished the flames, so he decided to attempt to reach his own lines instead. No news of his fate was received back at the base, however, and his colleagues were convinced that he was lost – 'Dziubek', known for his high spirits and sense of humour, was mourned throughout No 244 Wing. Then, to everyone's joy, he marched into the mess-tent the following morning as if nothing had happened. Horbaczewski had glided into Gabes and landed with little fuss, although the damage to his fighter had proven to be more serious than he had thought, so he spent the night there, unable to contact his unit.

During the campaign three Polish pilots added sufficient victories to their scores to become aces. As mentioned above, 'Dziubek' Horbaczewski was the first to do so, scoring his fifth kill on 2 April, and he was followed by Sgts Popek and Sztramko. Popek's fifth kill deserves to be detailed. On 28 April Flt Lt Król, Flg Off Sporny and Flt Sgts Popek and Sztramko were playing bridge (their favourite pass-time). The bidding went up, and on hearing Król's call of five no trumps, Popek (his opponent) doubled with a big smile. Sporny, Król's partner, lost his nerve and redoubled, adding, 'I'll teach you not to double your superiors!' By that time Król was perfectly aware that the game was lost, as he only had one ace on hand (co-incidentally, at that time he was the only *fighter* ace at the table, although Popek and Sztramko would join the 'club' soon, and Sporny scored his fifth in June 1944). With the stake taking on sizeable proportions, it was with relief that Król received an order to scramble.

Upon hearing the news of an operation, Popek put his cards into his pocket, which left no doubt amongst his opponents that, war or

Flg Off Bohdan Arct was an artist by profession, and between sorties he would take every opportunity to maintain his skills – even in the African desert. He paintings of the the latter theatre produced a colourful chronicle of the Polish pilots' African adventure (*Arct*)

'Skalski's Circus' is captured on film just at the point of scrambling on a sortie. EN315/ZX-6 was used by both Horbaczewski and Popek to score their respective fifth 'ace-making' kills, this Spitfire actually being more successful than any of its PFT masters by achieving no fewer six kills, two probables and two damaged whilst being flown by five different pilots – with a record like this it is little wonder that the Spitfire was flown by virtually every 'Circus' pilot, and also by No 145 Sqn's 'A' Flight Commander, Flt Lt Hesketh. The next Spitfire in line also exhibits swastikas beneath its cockpit, but seems to bear no codes whatsoever. In fact, three kills were scored with EN261 before the Spitfire received the code ZX-10 (*Cynk*)

not, he was not willing to give up a promising deal. In a short time they were patrolling over Bizerta, where Popek's luck held. During what must have seemed to him to have been merely a flying break between the bid and the play, he spotted a lone Macchi, chased it down and destroyed it. After an hour they returned to base, and the deal was played. Król and Sporny were three under, adding further to Popek's score!

In 40 days the team scored a total of 25 enemy aircraft confirmed destroyed, 3 probably destroyed and 9 damaged, for the loss of one pilot (made a PoW). PFT's last victories came on 6 May when Sztramko destroyed a Bf 109 (thus becoming an ace) and Skalski damaged another.

A week later Axis troops in North Africa surrendered, and the PFT was disbanded. It had been planned that the pilots would return to Britain to pass their experience on to others. However, Desert Air Force HQ was so impressed with the 'Skalski's Circus' that the Poles were asked to stay on in the Mediterranean in commanding positions with RAF units. Upon receiving this offer, Skalski mentioned that five of his pilots were NCOs, to which AVM Harry Broadhurst replied without hesitation, 'They could be flight lieutenants by tomorrow'. PAF HQ declared that the volunteers were free to accept the offer, and eventually three did – Skalski, Horbaczewski and Drecki. The latter had flown in combat since 1939, during which time he had officially destroyed three aircraft and damaged a fourth, although some sources claim he had scored more kills.

Horbaczewski was posted to No 43 Sqn, whilst Skalski and Drecki stayed with No 244 Wing. In mid-July Skalski took command of No 601 'County of London' Sqn, and what follows is a series of quotes from his pilots describing his ability as a fighter leader;

'We moved to Malta early in June and covered landings in Sicily in July. S/L Taylor was shot down and killed in the morning of the invasion on 10 July 1943, and S/L Skalski became CO a few days later. He was

Skalski strikes a pose alongside a suitably-marked No 601 Sqn truck during his time as the unit's commanding officer (*Drecki*)

with us for about two months until relieved by Major Osler – a South African – at Foggia, Italy. I knew S/L Skalski well, as he was with us for some time, and I flew as his number two on quite a few occasions. Everyone respected S/L Skalski. I considered him to be the best squadron leader that I flew with. I believe many others who were fortunate enough to fly with him would agree with me. One little anecdote I remember may illustrate how cool he was in the air. He was always very clear and precise in his instructions, which of course were in English. At that time we had two Belgians with us, one of whom was from the Congo. At times he got rather excited, and his English was never good. After one such incident Skalski commented, "Hagico, – if – you – do – not – speak – slowly – and – distinctly – I – cannot – understand – you". There was stunned silence for some time' – W M Matheson

'Sqn Ldr Skalski was renowned for letting his pilots have a go at getting a "kill" if the opportunity arose, instead of grabbing the glory himself. A good and respected leader' – W J Malone.

'S/Ldr Stanislaw Skalski was the OC of 601 when I joined, and left the squadron probably in late October 1943. He was an excellent leader and easy to fly with, as he never did unexpected manoeuvres and always kept his flight well informed. He was a quiet person who was well respected by us pilots of the Squadron' – New Zealander, Tom Ross.

Flg Off Drecki, meanwhile left No 244 Wing in August 1943 to become a flight commander with No 152 Sqn. One of his fellow pilots in that unit was Ron Bell, who describes the Pole in the following quote;

'Mike was a good man. Always smiling, always joking. He had more victories than he claimed(!) . . . Ingram (OC No 152 Sqn) brought him because we needed somebody with more tactical experience. He was always laughing – everything was a joke to him. He was telling us about his family in occupied Poland. He never gave orders, but rather asked you to do something.'

On 11 September 1943 Drecki downed a Bf 109. The unit had not scored a victory for some time, and the kill was something of a break-

EP689/UF-X was one of a number of Spitfires V flown by Skalski during his time with No 601 Sqn (*Arnold*)

MA289/UM-T was the Spitfire V used by Flt Lt Drecki to score his final kill on 11 September 1943 (*Drecki*)

through. Unfortunately, he was killed two days later in a take-off accident when a tyre burst after the wingtip of his Spitfire had hit another aircraft that had been parked too close to the runway.

Flt Lt Horbaczewski was posted to No 43 Sqn on 6 July 1943, also as a flight commander. One of his pilots, J Norby King, later recalled in his book *Green Kiwi Versus German Eagle*;

'He is slim and dark and quick. He has Polish gongs as well as a DFC, from intense experience in a Polish outfit with the Desert Air Force. "Horbaczewski" is a bit of a mouthful, so we call him "Horby".'

Fellow Kiwi Jack Torrance (who later formed, trained and led No 351 'Yugoslav' Sqn) explained;

'"Horby", as we called him, immediately injected a new spirit of aggression and confidence firstly into "A" Flight, and soon into the whole squadron. He called in fledgling pilots on several occasions to finish off enemy aircraft he had already damaged.'

This latter point is illustrated by No 43 Sqn's ORB entry for 27 July 1943, at 1245 hours;

'3 Spitfires attacked an ME 109 at 1000 ft which had just taken off. Enemy aircraft was seen to crash 1 mile South of aerodrome in flames and is claimed as destroyed. F/LT. E. HORBACZEWSKI, the first pilot to attack, foregoes his claim to share. ME.109 shared by P/O W. H. REID (CANADA) and F/SGT T. E. JOHNSON.'

On 9 August Horbaczewski was appointed OC No 43 Sqn, and the unit's ORB declared;

'We all feel fortunate in having S/Ldr Horbaczewski as our following Commanding Officer as we had got to know him as a Flight Commander, and appreciate his qualities very highly.'

J Norby King again;

'"Horby" introduces us to "Finger Four" sections so that the squadron of 12 can manoeuvre easily and watch out for each other's tails while looking towards the leader.'

And Jack Torrance;

Wg Cdr Skalski and Sqn Ldr Horbaczewski (proudly wearing his second DFC) are seen back in Britain soon after they had returned from the Mediterranean. Note the cross-shaped PFT badges on their pockets, above which Skalski also wears a No 601 Sqn badge (*Bargielowski*)

'I recall one occasion when a Hurricane crashed in flames on the runway and burnt. While most of us were interested in keeping out of the way of exploding ammunition, "Horby" was still trying to get at the pilot, who was hanging from his straps unconscious or dead, to get him out.'

On 4 September, whilst the unit was operating from Cassala, Horbaczewski destroyed a Bf 109, followed later that month by two kills whilst flying out of Falcone – on both occasions he used Spitfire VIII JF571/FT-13 (his only flights in the aircraft). He damaged an Fw 190 on the 15th, followed 24 hours later by two Focke-Wulf fighters destroyed.

Horbaczewski also enjoyed combating the Germans in less obvious ways too. On 1 October 1943 news spread through the squadron that Naples had fallen. As the unit had recently exhausted its wine stocks, and the only radio set capable of receiving the BBC had gone u/s, the OC (accompanied by the Intelligence Officer) took a jeep to look for these essential items. Once in the streets of the apparently liberated city, they were halted by a crowd of Italians. A discussion in a mixture of English, Italian and Polish revealed that the news of liberation was somewhat exaggerated, and in fact a German Tiger tank was in full control of the vicinity. Hardly deterred by this change of events, 'Horby' managed to locate a few Shermans of the 7th Armoured Division, and with their help, as well as that of the local inhabitants, dispose of the Tiger. Upon returning to the unit with the jeep's backseat full of 'shopping', Horbaczewski remarked that further news of Allied advances should better be verified!

By mid-October the unit was based at Capodichino. No 43 Sqn's Form 541 entry for the 13th stated;

'At 1000 hours we hear that S/Ldr E. Horbaczewski is posted – the whole Squadron is stunned. In the short time he had been with the Squadron he had endeared himself to all and was very highly respected by all, his energy, zeal and quiet but firm grip on the Squadron made him an ideal Squadron Commander. A farewell party was held in the Officers' Mess but was not as gay as usual because we all felt the shadow of "Horby's" departure. The following day S/Ldr Horbaczewski left at 0800 hours taking with him the good wishes of every member of the Squadron.'

US CONNECTION

WITH PIOTR WIŚNIEWSKI AND MICHAŁ MUCHA

In mid-June 1942 No 303 Sqn was posted from the hectic frontline fighter station at Northolt to the relative backwater of Kirton-in-Lindsey for a well-earned rest period. The latter airfield was also then home to the newly-arrived 94th Fighter Squadron (FS)/1st Fighter Group (FG) of the USAAF's Eighth Air Force, equipped with P-38 Lightnings. The Americans later commented in No 303 Sqn's chronicle;

'August 23, 1942 Kirton-in-Lindsey. Upon our arrival in England we were extremely pleased to hear we were to be stationed with the famous No 303 Sqn. It was with great anticipation that we landed at Kirton Lindsey on July 25, 1942. Almost immediately a strong bond of friendship sprang up between the Polish and American Squadrons, both among the officers and enlisted men. This friendship was greatly strengthened during our training, especially through many combats between the pilots, the numerous talks here and there, Horbaczewski deflection shooting, the Polish combat films, Zumbach instructions on formations and all the other pilots emphasizing on "looking, looking, always looking" and "continuous weaving". 303 helped us during our training.

'The loan of their sound advice on combat techniques, their explanation of their formation and beautiful examples of flying in thin gas which we believe will prove invaluable to us later on, and will be remembered and greatly appreciated by all members of our Squadron. Despite our imperfections our showing in the Group formation as the best Squadron is due largely to our association with 303. Although they gained more experience as photographers than combat pilots in our frequent dog-

An echelon formation of No 303 Sqn Spitfire VBs is seen in the summer of 1942. Nearest to the camera is BM540/RF-L, which Flt Lt Horbaczewski used for 'dogfighting with Lightnings at 30,000 ft', according to No 303 Sqn documents. At that time the PAF unit was based at Kirton-in-Lindsey along with the USAAF's 94th FS/1st FG (*Wandzilak*)

In late 1942 Capt Francis Gabreski was posted on an exchange tour to No 315 Sqn. His time with the unit helped him gain operational experience, refresh his Polish and make new friends among Polish Air Force pilots. Here, he is seen extricating himself from the cockpit of a No 315 Sqn Spitfire following the completion of a mission (*Koniarek*)

fights, we feel that we have learned a lot from them.'

Maj Glen E Hubbard, CO of the 94th FS, went on to add;

'During the short stay at Kirton-in-Lindsey the boys of 303 have done much to improve and to build up the 94th Squadron. For this I am very grateful, and I speak for us all when I say this. May we approach the fine record attained by the 303. We do not expect to beat it but we shall certainly try to equal this fine record.'

GABRESKI'S POLES

In late 1942 one Capt Francis Gabreski of the Eighth Air Force arrived in Britain. Thanks to his parentage he spoke Polish, and so duly applied for a posting to a Polish unit in order to acquire combat experience. He was sent to the Northolt Wing, where Wg Cdr Kołaczkowski assigned him to Sqn Ldr Tadeusz Sawicz's No 315 Sqn. Gabreski flew eleven combat and two ASR missions with this unit between December 1942 and February 1943, gaining invaluable operational experience and having many good times out of the cockpit at *Orchard's*, and elsewhere. He also developed a number of strong friendships with the Polish pilots.

Within a year Gabreski was commander of the P-47-equipped 61st FS within Hub Zemke's legendary 56th FG, seeing plenty of action escorting B-17s over Germany. Conversely, his chums at Northolt had hardly seen a German aircraft for months as they went about hitting ground targets as part of the 'softening of the Atlantic Wall' in preparation for D-Day. With pilots frustrated at the lack of aerial opposition, it therefore came as no surprise when several applied for an exchange posting to an American unit once they had completed their combat tours. The first to obtain such a posting was Wg Cdr Gabszewicz, who joined the 56th FG on 12 December 1943. Others, assuming that they would not be missed at staff posts in London, joined Gabreski's unit for occasional missions without any official sanction!

The latter group included Flg Off Tadeusz Andersz (who had taught 'Gabby' many 'tricks of the trade' during his No 315 Sqn days), Flt Lt Bolesław Gładych and Flt Lt Witold Łanowski. These pilots would all add further kills to their respective scores whilst flying P-47s over the coming months. Andersz eventually returned to a Polish squadron, but the unofficial status of the other two became known throughout the

USAAF, as well as the PAF, later in the year. Polish authorities attempted to discipline Gładych and Łanowski, who had caused headaches amongst the 'high brass' of the PAF on previous occasions, giving them the choice of resuming their official duties or being expelled from the service – both swiftly chose to fly fighters rather than desks, and thus had to leave the ranks of Poland's air arm. Remaining in P-47s, Gładych had downed ten enemy aircraft and Łanowski four by the end of 1944.

Although the staff at PAF HQ looked favourably upon the idea of sending airmen to fly with USAAF units in order to gain combat experience that could be useful after the war, the Eighth Air Force's strategic bombing role was not deemed to be relevant to the anticipated postwar mission of the Polish Air Force.

However, the tactically-optimised Ninth Air Force offered many more useful opportunities, and a number of officers were duly posted to its units, including aces Flt Lts Głowacki and Główczyński. The former, disappointed with staff paperwork, applied for a flying posting, and was given command of the PAF's No 309 Sqn in September 1944. Główczyński took a less official route to operational flying by obtaining a posting to the 366th FG, ostensibly to study logistical problems encountered whilst operating in the field! He would fly Thunderbolts with the 390th FS until the end of the war.

The Polish 'section' of the 61st FS/56th FG, Eighth Air Force. From left to right, Bolesław Gładych, Tadeusz Sawicz, Francis Gabreski, Kazimierz Rutkowski, Tadeusz Andersz and Witold Łanowski. Zbigniew Janicki, the sixth Polish pilot who flew with the unit during the spring of 1944, was killed on 13 June – prior to this photograph being taken (*Wagner via Stachyra*)

P-47D 42-26044/HV-Ż *Silver Lady* was flown with some success by both Gładych and Łanowski (*Wagner*)

The Mysterious Sobański

'In the 4th FG in England where I flew Spitfires, and which was formed from the Eagle Squadrons, was a Pole named Mike Sobański, who transferred from the RAF to the USAAF and became a US citizen. A nice guy, he spoke English with a Polish accent' – L W Chick, Jr, P-47 ace.

'Mike was room-mate and closest friend to me; probably the closest friend I ever had. After the war, I was persuaded to write a book, and I devoted a chapter to him' – James A Goodson, P-51 ace.

Born on 29 July 1919 to a Warsaw family, Wacław Michał Sobański was wounded in 1939 whilst serving in the infantry. In order to leave his German-occupied country, he managed to obtain an American passport through family connections. Arriving in the USA in the summer of 1940, Sobański went to Canada to join the RAF but failed his English exam, although after further study he managed to complete the flying training. Strange as it may seem, he would never serve with a PAF unit, although in May 1942 he spent brief periods with the RAF's Nos 132 and 164 Sqns, flying with Poles (in the latter unit he met 'Charlie' Blok).

With his new American citizenship, Sobański transferred to the Eighth Air Force and flew with the 4th FG, commanding the 334th FS from mid-April 1944 until his death on D-Day whilst leading the squadron on its second mission of the day. According to 4th FG documentation, he was credited with five and one shared kills (including one on the ground) – it is possible that his official USAAF score was later changed to five and two shared destroyed, three of which were ground kills.

Interestingly, Sobański must have known 'Dziubek' Horbaczewski, for the 4th FG held a party on 16 April 1944 at Debden to celebrate the

Maj Wacław Michał Sobański (or Winslow Michael Sobanski according to his USAAF documents) was photographed while commanding the 334th FS/4th FG in 1944 (*Konsler via Mucha*)

'Ches' Główczyński poses in front of *Blitz Buggy* – his personal P-47 within the 366th FG, Ninth Air Force (*Główczyński via Wagner*)

400th German aircraft to be claimed by the unit. That event was one of the few occasions specially marked in Horbaczewski's personal agenda, so it must have really been a party to remember.

URBANOWICZ VERSUS JAPAN

Although Poles had fought against Germany and Italy on virtually every front in Europe and the Mediterranean, the third Axis power received significantly less attention. In fact only one representative of the Polish nation actually took part in combat against Japan!

From June 1942 Maj Witold Urbanowicz had performed the role of assistant air attaché at the Polish Embassy in Washington. There, he met Col Cooper, who had founded the 'Kosciuszko' Squadron and whom he had already met in Britain in 1940. Cooper had also helped organise the American Volunteer Group (AVG) in China – the 'Flying Tigers' – and he introduced Urbanowicz to its commanding officer, Gen Claire Chennault. The Pole expressed his interest in flying with the AVG to the general, and in late 1943 he was posted in China – officially to gain operational experience in air support of ground operations. Initially, he

Maj Urbanowicz (right) and Maj Elmer W Richardson, CO of the 75th FS/23rd FG, are seen at Hengyang, in China, in December 1943 (*Lopez*)

flew with the 16th FS at Chengkung and the 74th FS at Kunming, then during November/December 1943, he completed a dozen missions (some 26 hours of flying hours) with the 75th FS at Hengyang.

On 11 January 1944 Maj-Gen Chennault awarded an Air Medal to Urbanowicz, the award's accompanying orders giving a brief description of the latter's activities in China;

'Major Urbanowicz distinguished himself by meritorious achievement in aerial fighting during his voluntary service with squadrons of the United States Army Air Forces in China from 23 October 1943 to 15 December 1943. During this period he participated as a pilot of fighter aircraft in low level strafing, bombing, and escort missions involving approximately thirty four hours of combat flying. The majority of his missions were flown in support of Chinese ground forces when those forces were hard pressed by the Japanese in the Tungting Lake area. On December 11, 1943 he engaged in an attack on a Japanese formation returning to its base and, in the ensuing air battle, brought down two enemy fighter planes. Throughout his combat service he displayed courage and fighting skill in the face of the enemy. His actions reflected credit on his personal record as well as that of the Polish and United States Armed Forces.'

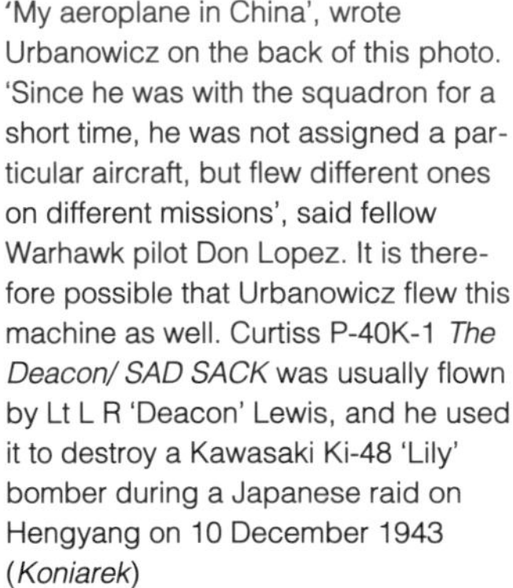

'My aeroplane in China', wrote Urbanowicz on the back of this photo. 'Since he was with the squadron for a short time, he was not assigned a particular aircraft, but flew different ones on different missions', said fellow Warhawk pilot Don Lopez. It is therefore possible that Urbanowicz flew this machine as well. Curtiss P-40K-1 *The Deacon/ SAD SACK* was usually flown by Lt L R 'Deacon' Lewis, and he used it to destroy a Kawasaki Ki-48 'Lily' bomber during a Japanese raid on Hengyang on 10 December 1943 (*Koniarek*)

INVASION AND ON

WITH MICHAŁ MUCHA

Late in 1943 PFT veterans Sqn Ldrs Skalski and Horbaczewski left their RAF units in the Mediterranean and returned to Britain – the 2nd Tactical Air Force (TAF) was forming in preparation for D-Day, and every experienced fighter leader was needed within the PAF.

Elsewhere, on 20 February 1944 Grp Capt Gabszewicz succeeded Grp Capt Tadeusz Rolski as OC No 18 (Polish) Sector, RAF. By D-Day this sector comprised three wings – Nos 131 (previously 1st Polish) and 135 (British, Belgian, and New Zealand squadrons) with Spitfires, and the Mustang-equipped No 133 (2nd Polish). Thus, in the early weeks of invasion Gabszewicz would lead an Allied air force twice the size of the *Brygada Pościgowa* in which he had started the war in September 1939.

Skalski was promoted to take command of No 131 Wing and 'Roch' Kowalski No 133 Wing, although in early 1944 the two men swapped after it was decided that the latter wing would have one British unit (No 129 Sqn) attached – Kowalski had no experience in leading British-manned squadrons. Skalski soon exercised his authority upon taking command of the wing when he had to instruct Murmansk veteran Sqn Ldr 'Wag' Haw (OC No 129 Sqn) to remove his Order of Lenin from his tunic so as to avoid any unpleasantness between the veteran ace and his new Polish wing-mates! Skalski encountered no such problems with his other squadron commanders – No 315 Sqn was led by 'Dziubek' Horbaczewski and No 306 Sqn by Stanisław Łapka, the latter pilot being an old schoolmate from Dęblin. When Skalski's tour ended in July, he was replaced by another Dęblin friend (and ace), 'Johann' Zumbach.

No 306 Sqn would become the second top-scoring Polish unit of 1944, being credited with 23 kills. Three of its pilots became aces during June

As Wing Commander Flying No 133 (Polish) Wing, Stanisław Skalski used Mustang III FZ152/SS for mush of 1944. It is seen here in full invasion stripes just after D-Day (*Cynk*)

This frame was taken from the ciné-camera film shot by Sgt Bargiełowski whilst flying Mustang III FB145/PK-F on 12 June 1944. It shows the final moments of one of two Fw 190s downed by him on this day south of Caen (*Bargielowski*)

1944 – Flt Lt Potocki (credited with his first victory just a month before) gained his fifth and sixth kills on 23 June, whilst Flt Lts Sporny and Sołogub (who had opened their scores in September 1941 with Nos 302 and 306 Sqns respectively) got their fifth kills on 23 and 24 June .

Topping the PAF kill tally by quite some margin in 1944 was Horbaczewski No 315 Sqn, which commenced its run of success with the Mustang III on 25 May by shooting down two Arado Ar 96s. The following month a further 13 German fighters were destroyed.

June 1944 also witnessed an example of just how much 'Dziubek' cared for his men. On the 22nd Sgt Tamowicz crash-landed in no-man's land during a sortie over the frontline. Ignoring his own safety, the OC swiftly landed his Mustang on an unfinished airfield, extricated the wounded pilot from his fallen fighter, and flew him back to base. No 133 Wing records summed the episode up in a single line – 'S/Ldr Horbaczewski brought back Sgt Tamowicz, naked and rather worn, but still usable'.

July brought a halt to offensive patrols as No 133 Wing was assigned to anti-'Diver' (V1) missions. Even then 'Dziubek' Horbaczewski provided his squadron with the opportunity of a kill on an occasional mission to Normandy or . . . Norway.

Flt Lt Janusz Lewkowicz poses by the Mustang I (AG648) in which he flew his 'illegally' successful long-range mission to Norway in 1942, thus paving the way for many aces to hunt in Scandinavian skies in later years (*Gronostaj*)

No 315 Sqn pilots pose at Brenzett after the mission to Norway on 30 July 1944 that had seen five of them claim seven German fighters destroyed. They are, from left to right, Plt Off Świstuń, Sqn Ldr Horbaczewski, Flg Off Nowosielski, Flt Lt Cwynar and Flt Sgts Jankowski and Będkowski. Note that Horbaczewski wears an American-style life vest, rather than the more bulky RAF type worn by the others. He probably 'acquired' it at the party held by the Eighth Air Force's 4th FG at Debden in April 1944 – fellow-Pole Maj Sobański was flying with the 4th FG at that time (*Bargiełowski*)

The latter destination for a unit based in the south-east of England deserves an explanation. Back in 1942 No 309 Sqn Mustang I pilot Flt Lt Lewkowicz (who, incidentally never scored a single kill) calculated that his aircraft could get to Norway and back with a reasonable fuel reserve. Although he had a degree in aircraft design, and his calculations had been meticulously worked out, Lewkowicz's report on his discovery failed to get through the bureaucratic machine. So, on 27 September 1942 he took off for a 'weather test' and set course across the North Sea. After attacking targets of opportunity near Stavanger, he returned safely. This sortie earned him a reprimand for unauthorised action, but prompted the RAF to commence Mustang missions across the North Sea.

Returning to 1944, on 30 July No 315 Sqn flew just such a mission to Norway, during which Flt Lt Cwynar 'made ace'. He later recalled;

'As we approached the Wash, the weather began to close in with a rainy, warm frontal system approaching from the west. We soon spotted the Canadian Beaufighters, in close formation, low down, "on the deck", to avoid radar detection. The weather worsened rapidly as we closed in on the Beaufighters, forming a tight formation around the Canadians, whose leader kept a steady course while "hugging the waves".

'After two hours of total concentration, suddenly it was as if we had flown through a curtain or passed over a cliff. There was a complete transformation. We had overtaken the eastern edge of the frontal system. The sun was behind us – a useful tactical advantage – and in front we had the beautiful panoramic view of the Norwegian coast.

'Within a few minutes one of Horbaczewski's wingmen spotted German fighters approaching through a fjord's inlet, heading for the Beaufighters. There were two groups of four Bf 109s, leisurely, almost nonchalantly, carrying out a left-hand turn in order to take up position to attack the Canadians. Jettisoning our wing fuel tanks, we attacked. Horbaczewski went in first, attacking the inner group, and I engaged the outer formation.

'In diving and then climbing in a left-hand turn I had engaged the group's leader. By the way he was scything through the air, the edges of his Messerschmitt's wings stitching the sky with air-condensed threads, I realised he was good. He pulled hard – so did I! With the fuselage fuel tank still full and the Mustang's adverse lateral stability, there wasn't much room for imagi-

Sqn Ldr 'Dziubek' Horbaczewski is seen about to sign his aircraft's maintenance check list prior to starting FB166 up. Note the yellow and black horizontal striping on the inboard portion of the flap leading edge, which served as a flap deflection indicator. No 315 Sqn pilots developed the technique of extending the flaps by 10° in order to enhance low-speed manoeuvrability (Bargiełowski)

No 302 Sqn Spitfires are seen at Vendeville airfield, in France, during the summer of 1944. ML124/WX-E was flown by several aces, including Sqn Ldr Król and Flt Lt Gnyś, whilst MJ783/WX-F was apparently used on occasion by Grp Capt Gabszewicz, OC No 131 Wing. ML358/WX-H was also flown by Gabszewicz, as well as fellow ace Flt Lt Sołogub. Despite flying Spitfire IXs, and boasting many skilled aces, No 302 Sqn failed to score any kills during 1944, instead being primarily employed on ground attack duties (*Cynk*)

native manoeuvring, so I had to hold a steady, smooth turn. With a few hundred revs always in reserve, I held on patiently. For one 360° circle or more there was stalemate. Then I lowered flaps 10° and was gaining on him. My solar plexus stopped churning as I felt sure of getting on his tail, all the time thinking "Pull smoothly. Get that extra reserve throttle on". I got him in my gunsight's illuminated ring, pulled straight through his line of flight, one diameter . . . two . . . three diameters of deflection and then pressed the firing button. For a split second there was nothing, then I saw bullets punching holes, first on his tail section, and then on the fuselage, canopy, wings . . .'

During the combat six Mustangs downed eight German fighters, and subsequent sorties to the Norwegian coast continued into 1945 – indeed, one such mission on 7 December saw Sgt Bargiełowski claim his fifth kill.

No 315 Sqn's next memorable action actually resulted in the unit being credited with the highest number of kills scored by an RAF squadron in a single sortie. The date was 18 August 1944, and the action occurred when 12 PK-coded Mustang IIIs on a morning sweep encountered a formation of 60 Fw 190s assembling near Beauvais. In the ensuing melée, three German fighters fell to both Sqn Ldr Horbaczewski – who sadly failed to return from the mission – and Flt Sgt Siwek (these were his only victories of the war). Ace Flt Lt Henryk Pietrzak was credited with two and one shared kills, while Flt Sgt Bargielowski also destroyed a pair of Fw 190s and damaged a further two. The unit was finally credited with 16 kills in

Following the re-organisation of the RAF in mid-July 1944, which has seen the system of operational sectors abandoned, Grp Capt Gabszewicz took command of No 131 Wing (which combined the previous No 131 Wing and Airfield No 131). Gabszewicz's Spitfire IX NH214/SZ-G *CITY of WARSAW* is seen here at an airfield (possibly in liberated Belgium) during November 1944. Rather than apply his initials to the aircraft – as was common practice amongst senior RAF pilots at that time – Gabszewicz chose the code SZ-G, for he had used it when flying with No 316 'City of Warsaw' Sqn in 1941/42. Note the unit badge just visible behind the cockpit, and the name of the squadron on the cowling immediately in front of the windscreen. Although No 316 Sqn still used SZ codes in 1944, it had converted to Mustang IIIs by that time, so there was no risk of mistaking the Spitfire's identity when on No 131 Wing operations – especially with the group captain's pennant prominently displayed beneath the cockpit. The boxing dog motif was also repeated on several of Gabszewicz's Spitfires (*Cynk*)

Although assigned to the Air Defence of Great Britain, No 316 Sqn was also employed on ground attack duties, as graphically shown by this photograph of a bomb fitted beneath the wing of a squadron Mustang III. Sitting on its wheel is Wt Off Aleksander Pietrzak (not to be confused with the then Flt Lt Henryk Pietrzak of No 315 Sqn). Pietrzak was one of the unit's V1 aces, achieving a score of four and one shared V1s. He also claimed three and one shared German fighters destroyed, plus two damaged (including an Me 262). This Mustang III is possibly that of Wt Off Tadeusz Szymański, whose final score would reach two Fw 190s confirmed destroyed and one damaged, plus eight V1s destroyed

total, with apparently no – or at least very little – overclaiming, for the combined total of Allied victories for that day (35 confirmed kills) was almost identical to the total losses (32) admitted by *Jagdkorps II*. No 315 Sqn's opponents had been II./JG 26, and probably either I./JG 2 or III./JG 2. The combat at Beauvais cost the former *Gruppe* eight aircraft destroyed and one 28 per cent damaged, with seven pilots killed and one badly wounded. JG 2 lost 11 aircraft, its *III.Gruppe* suffering such heavy casualties that it was immediately ordered back to Germany.

'Doodlebug' Hunting

Although less glamourous than fighting against the Luftwaffe, the pursuit of V1 flying bombs was no less important. The first two 'divers' credited to a Polish pilot were downed on 16 June 1944 by Sgt Domański, flying

This photograph shows Ghent airfield in the aftermath of the surprise German attack on the morning of 1 January 1945 (Operation *Bodenplatte*). Seen in the background, behind the wrecked Spitfire, is Gabszewicz's Mk IX NH214/SZ-G (*Sembrat*)

Flg Off Tadeusz Szlenkier was one of the young Polish pilots who claimed their first (and last) aerial victories of the war on that New Year's morning. He is standing here by the wreck of an Fw 190 he had shot down (*Bochniak*)

a Tempest V with No 3 Sqn, RAF. Soon, all three Polish Mustang III units were carrying out this role, with No 316 Sqn (as part of the force assigned the Air Defence of Great Britain) emerging as the most successful PAF anti-'diver' unit with 64 single and 22 shared kills – this figure was officially calculated to 74 and 5/12ths. No 306 Sqn scored 43 and 36 shared (59 and 7/12ths) and No 315 Sqn 36 and 40 shared (54 1/2). No 133 Wing's HQ flight was also credited with a solitary V1, downed by Grp Capt Nowierski.

The largest V1 haul was achieved on 20 July, when Polish squadrons brought down 20 'buzz-bombs' – 15 days earlier No 316 Sqn had destroyed seven of these weapons. Although it was the latter unit which excelled in this role, the three PAF V1 top-scorers all came from No 306 Sqn. Flt Sgt Rudowski and Flt Lt Siekierski were both credited with seven and three shared apiece (officially calculated as 8 1/2 and 8 and 1/6th), while Flt Sgt Józef Zaleński got five and six shared (8). Wt Off Szymański of No 316 Sqn destroyed eight 'divers', while Flt Sgt Jankowski of No 315 Sqn added four and four shared (officially six in total) to his score – both pilots were V1 top-scorers in their respective units. With the exception of Flt Sgt Zaleński, each of the pilots listed above also claimed aircraft kills, although none was an ace. Only three pilots would achieve such a distinction in respect to both aircraft and V1s destroyed, and they all served with No 315 Sqn – Sqn Ldr Horbaczewski and Flt Lt's Henryk Pietrzak and Cwynar.

Although No 316 Sqn was mainly employed on anti-'diver' duties, it occasionally flew operations over the continent. These intensified as the V1 attacks ceased, and on midday on 18 October 1944, six of its Mustangs encountered an equal number of Bf 109s over the North Sea and shot them all down. One of the sortie's victors was No 133 Wing Leader (and ace) Wg Cdr Rutkowski, who claimed a shared kill. Also credited with victories were two V1 aces, namely Flt Lt Stefan Karnkowski and Wt Off Aleksander Pietrzak. A further two Bf 109s were claimed by Flt Lt Janusz Walawski, who narrowly missed becoming an ace with four confirmed kills and three damaged.

Aces Wg Cdr Rutkowski (left) and Flt Lt Łokuciewski are seen soon after the latter's release from a PoW camp. Rutkowski scored five kills, a probable and a damaged with Nos 306 and 317 Sqns. Near the end of the war he added a shared kill and a probable whilst flying Mustang IIIs as Wing Commander Flying No 133 Wing. 'Tolo' Łokuciewski had scored a kill in the Battle of France, four in the Battle of Britain and three more in the summer 1941 (all seven with No 303 Sqn) by the time he was shot down and captured by the Germans on 13 March 1942. In 1945 he became No 303 Sqn's last OC, and had the sad privilege of disbanding the most famous of all Polish squadrons (*Bargiełowski*)

Due to the shorter range of its Spitfires, No 131 Wing would subsequently become the first (and

Although the quality of this photograph is far from perfect, it is the only known in-flight shot showing a mixed formation of No 303 Sqn's natural-metal Mk IVA and camouflaged Mk IV Mustangs. The unit's well known RF codes gave way to PD in August 1945

only) Polish wing based on the continent, where it was used for ground support, and therefore had few opportunities to engage enemy aircraft.

By this stage of the war, many PAF fighter pilots had commenced combat flying in 1943/44, by which time the Luftwaffe was a shadow of its former self. The 'new' pilots could only envy the air battles fought on a daily basis by their slightly older colleagues during the Battle of Britain, when dozens of enemy fighters and bombers were engaged. Some of these veterans were now their commanders – men like ace Grp Capt Gabszewicz, who commanded No 131 Wing (after the RAF had disbanded all sectors) through France and into Belgium. He would finish the war with the wing at Ahlhorn, in Germany, where he was replaced in mid-1945 by Battle of Britain ace Grp Capt Witorzeńć. The wing's squadrons would also be commanded at times by such legendary pilots as Sqn Ldrs Król, Gnyś and Pniak, all of whom had opened their scores in 1939.

When, on the morning of New Year's Day 1945, Sqn Ldr Marian Chełmecki of No 317 Sqn led his young pilots to bomb yet another target, little did he know that in a couple of hours they would re-live those hectic days of 1940 when he flew Hurricanes with No 17 Sqn. Upon returning from the mission, two of the wing's squadrons (the other being No 308 Sqn) found German *Jabos* bombing and strafing their airfield at Ghent-St Denijs Westrem, in Belgium. In 20 minutes, 18 PAF fighters destroyed 18 and one shared Fw 190s for the loss of just two aircraft downed by the Germans. Although the PAF's last true air battle had not involved any aces, it had given young pilots the opportunity to prove that they were just as good as their 'seniors'.

Of all the Polish aces, Jakub Bargiełowski was the last to open his score. Captured by the Soviets in 1939, he suffered the horrors of Stalin's *gulags* until released in mid-1941 following the German invasion of the USSR. Bargiełowski then came to Britain, and following conversion training, was posted to No 315 Sqn. He was subsequently credited with all five of his victories whilst flying with this unit in 1944. The following year he transferred to No 303 Sqn, where he remained until the unit's disbandment (*Bargiełowski*)

No 309 Sqn Mustang III WC-W probably wore the serial FB385 beneath its white fuselage band, which meant that it was the aircraft flown by Wt Off Murkowski on 9 April 1945 when he was credited with the destruction of an Me 262, plus the damaging of a second jet. This action was the last successful air combat experienced by any PAF squadron within the RAF. The Soviet-controlled 'People's Polish Air Force' would encounter Luftwaffe aircraft as late as May, however (*Fleischer*)

Wt Off Antoni Murkowski is seen in the cockpit of his Mustang III soon after the end of the war in Europe. Note the No 309 Sqn emblem to the left of his impressive scoreboard. Black crosses with outlines in different colours (following Wg Cdr Zumbach's pattern) stand for three kills, a probable and a damaged, whilst the four swastikas denote V1s destroyed (*Cynk*)

The Disney-inspired boxing dog, as seen on Spitfire XVI TD240/SZ-G – the last of Gabszewicz's aircraft during his time as OC No 131 Wing. A similar motif appeared in the badge of the USAAF's 62nd FS/56th FG, as well as several other American units (*Cynk*)

PAF fighter units continued their efforts until the end of the war, with the last kills scored by an ace being credited to Flt Lt Blok on 21 February 1945. In March and April encounters with German jets also occurred, and some Me 262s were downed. 25 April 1945 saw a most rewarding mission flown when PAF fighters (including Mustang IVs of the recently re-equipped No 303 Sqn) escorted 255 Lancasters sent to bomb Hitler's resort at Berchtesgaden. Their joy was not as unbridled as one might have thought, however, for the Poles were fully aware by now that, unlike every other Allied air forces in exile, they would not return to their homeland with their arms. Indeed, most of them would never return at all.

When the news of the Yalta Agreement had been announced in early 1945, it was a terrible blow for all Poles, for although it had been obvious that some sort of deal with Stalin had to be made, few had imagined that Western politicians would give him virtually a free hand in Poland. It was felt that five years of great sacrifice had been for nothing, as Nazi occupants had simply been replaced by communists. Then Flt Lt T E Johnson witnessed PAF Spitfire squadron personnel receive the contents of a letter sent by the British Foreign Secretary to all Polish units;

'To all intents and purposes it said "Thank you for your contribution to our victory. I am sorry you cannot come to England. You are forthwith released from duty . . ." It is the only time in my life that "politics" in its stark inhumanity caused me an anguish I have no desire to experience again. I was 23 years old. Can you imagine what I felt!? I stood by the side of my brother in arms and cursed my government!'

Polish veterans remember another British officer saying, 'Never before were there so many betrayed by so few, and for so little'.

Wg Cdr Tadeusz Sawicz – No 131 Wing's Wing Commander Flying – followed the example of his long-time friend Aleksander Gabszewicz by having his personal Spitfires coded in remembrance of his No 316 Sqn days. The last of these, Mk XVI TD238/SZ-K, was later flown by Wg Cdr Król after the latter pilot had assumed command of the wing. Król had the letters changed into his personal code, WK-L (*Zimny*)

Whilst based at Ahlhorn, in Germany, Polish pilots had plenty of time to pick through the wrecks of the latest German aircraft left abandoned by the defeated Luftwaffe. Here, Grp Capt Witorzeńć (OC No 131 Wing in late 1945) is seen standing by Me 262A-2a Wk-Nr 170070, which bears the dual markings of *Erprobungsstelle Rechlin* (E7+02) and KG(J) 51 (white 12)

Although No 318 Sqn was officially a fighter-reconnaissance unit, it was employed exclusively on tactical recce duties in Italy, and thus failed to score a single aerial kill. Despite its lack of success in the air as a fighter squadron, it was the only PAF unit to boast a Bf 109 in its inventory! In 1945 a perfectly serviceable ex-Croat *Gustav* was acquired from US troops for . . . a bottle of whisky – the Bf 109G subsequently gave Polish pilots much more fun than it had cost! It is seen here, complete with squadron codes, RAF roundel and fin flash and a PAF marking on the nose, at Treviso, in Italy, in March 1946 (*Thomas via Mucha*)

Every PAF pilot fought hoping for a glorious return to Warsaw, but not a single pilot was given the chance to land his aircraft there following VE-Day. When three PAF Spitfire XVIs (including TB292/QH-Z from No 302 Sqn, seen here at Warsaw-Okźcie airport in October) were eventually sent to the Polish capital for an RAF exhibition in 1945, they had to be delivered by RAF pilots, for active Polish Air Force personnel were not allowed to set foot on communist-controlled Polish soil! (*Stachyra*)

WHATEVER HAPPENED TO THE HEROES?

This chapter gives the biographies of the five top scoring Polish aces in the order of their official scores with the PAF.

SKALSKI – BLOOD, SWEAT AND TEARS

'S/L Skalski was an outstanding fighter pilot and leader. He was always a very careful pilot and never did anything flash or reckless, but was aggressive in action. He taught me how to see what was going on in the air. He seemed to know what was going on around us at all times, and must have had very good eyes' – that is how Stanisław Skalski is remembered by W M Matheson, one of his pilots in No 601 'County of London' Sqn.

Born in 1915 in Kodyma, Skalski joined the Dęblin school in 1936 and was commissioned in August 1938. He was then posted to *142 Eskadra* at Toruń. Credited with four and one shared victories, Skalski emerged as the only ace of the 1939 campaign. Escaping through Rumania and the Mediterranean, he arrived in France, and in early 1940 volunteered for service in Britain. Skalski served with No 501 Sqn during the Battle of Britain, after which he was posted to No 306 Sqn, before becoming OC of No 317 Sqn. Appointed PFT leader, he subsequently commanded No 601 Sqn, RAF, before returning to Britain, where he was given control of No 133 Wing in time for D-Day. Finishing his tour in September 1944, he was posted to the Command and General Staff School in the USA.

Following VE-Day, Skalski was offered a prominent post within the RAF, but he chose to return to Poland – regardless of the fact that his country was now controlled by the Soviets. Initially, he served in the communist-controlled Polish Air Force.

However, once the 'Cold War' got into full swing he was arrested and accused of spying for the 'American and British imperialists' – this happened to many wartime PAF pilots who had returned home from the West. Skalski subsequently underwent a terrible 'investigation' which matched the cruelty of anything the Gestapo or NKVD could have performed. Lucky to survive this inhuman treatment, he was then sentenced to death following the most absurd accusations. Eventually, the communists 'mercifully' changed the sentence to life imprisonment. Following Stalin's death in 1953, things began to slowly change in Poland, and in 1956 Skalski was released after eight years in prison.

He was quickly offered a job within the Polish Air Force, and after some hesitation, he accepted. Skalski subsequently had the opportunity to fly MiG jet fighters and other types, remaining a high-ranking officer (he eventually attained the rank of *generał brygady*) in the PAF until the

Sqn Ldr Skalski, photographed in 1942 while serving as OC No 317 Sqn (*Wandzilak*)

1970s. Skalski then headed the Polish Aero Club, and today, he still lives in Warsaw.

Stanisław Skalski is seen surrounded by other ex-wartime PAF pilots during jet training on MiG-15UTIs in 1957. Standing (left to right) are Łokuciewski, Skalski and Król, whilst sat in the rear cockpit is Ignacy Olszewski, who had commanded No 302 Sqn and then No 308 Sqn at war's end (*Olszewski*)

Urbanowicz – Gentleman Hero

'I knew Major Urbanowicz fairly well considering he was a Major and I was a Second Lieutenant at the time. He was very highly regarded by the squadron members, both as a man and as an outstanding fighter pilot. I had only a few combat missions at the time and was amazed at how much of what occurred in an air battle he was able to report compared with what the rest of us saw. Later, when I was a veteran of many combats, I was able to see and report a lot more but I was never able to reach his level of expertise. In the evenings we would enjoy listening to his stories of combat in the Battle of Britain' – these words were written by ace Donald S Lopez, who served with the 75th FS/23rd FG, USAAF, in China. He is now Deputy Director at the National Air and Space Museum in Washington, DC.

Witold Urbanowicz was born in 1908 in north-eastern Poland. He joined SPL at Dęblin in 1930 and was commissioned in 1932 as *podporucznik obserwator*, whereupon he was posted to night bomber squadron *1 Pułk Lotniczy*. He then applied for flying training, which he completed in 1933. After service with *111* and *113 Eskadras* he became and instructor at Dęblin, where he remained until the outbreak of war. In 1939 Urbanowicz was head of the '14 Promotion' class, and he nursed his entire group of cadet-officers through Rumania, and by sea, to Marseilles.

He then volunteered for training in Britain, and in August 1940 was posted firstly to No 601 Sqn, and then to 145 Sqn. Eventually Urbanowicz joined No 303 Sqn, where he assumed command of the unit after Sqn Ldr Krasnodębski had been badly burnt on 7 September. With 15 confirmed victories, he was by far the most successful Polish pilot of the Battle of Britain (no other Pole scored more than eight kills during the same period) . . . and he was the ripe old age of 32 at the time!

In 1941 Urbanowicz organised the Northolt Wing, subsequently lead ing it for a while. Having completed his RAF tour, and passed control of the wing over to Wg Cdr Piotr Łaguna, Urbanowicz left for the USA in June of that year. Once in America, he commenced a PAF publicity tour, giving lectures on fighter tactics in the European conflict. Upon its completion, Urbanowicz was appointed assistant air attaché at the Polish Embassy, but he soon grew bored with diplomacy and duly volunteered for service in China, where he spent a few months. In 1944 he returned to Washington once again as the Polish air attaché. Unlike many of his colleagues, Urbanowicz was never officially released from RAF duty once the war ended, being placed on permanent leave from July 1945 instead!

Ppłk Urbanowicz is seen at the end of World War 2. Note the Chinese pilot's wings above the right breast pocket of his battle dress (*Koniarek*)

That same year he returned to Poland just as the communists were doing their best to attract war heroes back to their homeland in order to prove the nation's 'normalisation' to the rest of the world. Upon his arrival he was arrested in error, but released after one day of imprisonment. This experience was enough to discourage any further thought of re-settling in Poland, however, and Urbanowicz duly emigrated to the USA, where he worked in the aerospace industry.

After the fall of communism he returned to Poland several times, being promoted to *generał* in 1995. In May of the following year he visited *1 Pułk Lotnictwa Myśliwskiego 'Warszawa'* on the 75th anniversary of the formation of his original pre-war unit – *1 Pułk Lotniczy* – in Warsaw. During this heart-warming ceremony the veteran ace gave his blessing to young fighter pilots, having finally 'come home' after 50 years in exile. Witold Urbanowicz died upon his return to the USA a few weeks later.

This informal photograph of Flt Lt Gładych was taken during his time as commander of 'B' Flight, No 302 Sqn, in late 1943. *PENGIE* was his personal Spitfire IX (MH906), and was probably coded WX-M (*Zieliński*)

HORBACZEWSKI – YOUNG FOREVER

'In every bunch of mail, sometimes in a pub conversation on leave, there is news of someone known, a friend, gone . . . "Horby" was killed in France leading a Polish flight, his Mustangs outnumbered. If I have to go it would have been good to have gone with him' – J Norby King, *Green Kiwi Versus German Eagle.*

Eugeniusz Horbaczewski was born in 1917 in Kiev. He was known throughout his life as 'Dziubek' (an informal Polish word which in English means 'darling' or 'kid'). He joined the SPL Dęblin in 1938, and was commissioned in the 13th Promotion on 1 September 1939.

Upon reaching France, Horbaczewski apparently flew with a Polish flight at Bordeaux before fleeing once again to Britain in June 1940 and obtaining a posting to No 303 Sqn. Always ready for action, he was a tough subordinate, and in September 1942 Sqn Ldr Zumbach had him posted away to No 302 Sqn following a series of minor incidents which eventually resulted in a Spitfire being written off. Apparently it was then that 'Dziubek' swore he would exceed Zumbach's score!

Horbaczewski then joined the PFT, and in six months scored eight kills in the Mediterranean, rising from flying officer to OC No 43 Sqn, RAF.

'"Horby" took us over and moulded us into one. He gave us a new confidence in the air, a new squadron formation and a new elan' – J N King.

Upon returning to Britain, Horbaczewski was made OC No 315 Sqn within No 133 Wing, led by Skalski. Ironically, in mid-1944 'Dziubek' found himself under the command of Zumbach once again after the latter replaced Skalski as Wing Leader – further irony was provided when Horbaczewski finally fulfilled his oath soon after the command change.

'Dziubek' was killed on 18 August 1944 during an air battle which saw his squadron credited with 16 Fw 190s destroyed – he downed three of them prior to his death. He was unwell that day, and some witnesses claim that he knew he would not survive an encounter with German fighters.

No 43 Sqn pilot T E Johnson remembers how Horbaczewski had said to his pilots, 'after we have finished here you will come and fight for my country – my country may not be free'. By the time of his death, the Soviets already controlled a large chunk of pre-war Poland, and were executing Polish patriots or sending them to Siberia – despite this, Stalin still enjoyed friendly relations with the West. It had become obvious to Horbaczewski that his homeland would not be free, so perhaps he chose to die, rather than face such a tragic postwar dilemma?

Gładych – *Enfant Terrible*

Born in 1918 in Warsaw, Bolesław Gładych was expelled from several schools in his formative years, before finally choosing a military career and joining the Dęblin school in 1938 . Commissioned on 1 September 1939, he failed to see combat in Poland and wound up in France with GC I/145 *Varsovie.*

Fleeing to Britain in June 1940, Gładych joined No 303 Sqn in April 1941. On 23 June he was credited with three kills in a day, but was seriously wounded and declared unfit for flying for a long period. He then served with No 302 Sqn, becoming a flight commander in late 1943.

A trio of future No 303 Sqn aces are seen on parade (probably at Northolt) in 1941. They are, from left to right, Plt Offs 'Gandhi' Drobiński, Gładych and Horbaczewski. All three men had previously been members of the 13th Promotion at Dęblin

From early 1944 onwards Gładych flew with the USAAF's 56th FG, and after receiving an ultimatum from PAF HQ in respect to his allegiance, he chose to fly with the Americans, and was consequently expelled from the PAF. Strange as it may seem, although he was a double ace with the USAAF, he was never officially in American service. In fact all Gładych's flying with the 56th FG was done 'just for the fun of it', if not as a mercenary!

After the war Gładych remained 'unofficially' attached to Amercian units in Britain, becoming involved in illegal activities. Subsequently, he emigrated to the USA, where he worked for a while in the aerospace industry. At the same time he wrote numerous articles describing his wartime exploits – some true, some untrue, but all invariably exciting.

Having subsequently obtained a degree in psychology in America, Gładych now works as a doctor in Seattle, Washington. When recently asked about his wartime experiences, he replied with astonishment, 'Who would care now? That was so long ago . . .'

Stern-faced Flt Lt *Gładych* (left) and smiling PAF Inspector, Grp Capt Mateusz Iżycki, are seen together in late 1943. Note the PFT badge that the latter officer had received following his tour as PAF Liaison Officer to the RAF in the Middle East during 'Skalski's Circus' operations earlier that same year. Gładych's score of seven kills is marked on his scarf – the trio of crosses lacking white borders denote two probables and a shared damaged claim (*Kopański*)

Zumbach – The Adventurer

Before work on this book started, it was decided that no foreign aces who flew with Polish units would be included, be they Czech, Canadian or Soviet. However, an exception to that rule had to be made for Jan Zumbach, for although born in Warsaw in 1915, he inherited Swiss

Horbaczewski scored most of his victories flying Spitfires of various marks. Here, he is seen as a pilot officer sat in a No 303 Sqn Mk V (*IV LO Zielona Góra*)

Sqn Ldr Jan Zumbach is seen in his Spitfire VB EP594/RF-D. The photograph was taken after Operation *Jubilee* (the Dieppe landings) on 19 August 1942, when he increased his score by one and one shared kills, plus a probable (compare the scoreboard seen here with the example shown in the colour photograph on the back cover – the latter shot was taken in May 1942, and features Zumbach's earlier *Donald Duck*, BM144) (*Chołoniewski*)

Swiss citizen Jean Zumbach was photographed in Zürich in 1956 – at about the time he gave up smuggling and became a restaurateur in Paris. Five years later he would change occupations once again, becoming mercenary 'Mr John Brown' of the Katangese Air Force *(via Stachyra)*

citizenship from his father. In 1936 he forged some documents in order to pass as a Pole, and subsequently join the Polish Armed Forces.

A cadet officer at SPL Dęblin, Zumbach was commissioned in 1938 (together with Stanisław Skalski) and posted to *111 Eskadra*. Wounded in an accident, he failed to participate in the 1939 campaign, although he saw combat in France with ECD I/55. Upon his arrival in Britain, Zumbach became a founder member of No 303 Sqn, going on to score all of his victories, bar one probable, with the unit. He then led the 3rd Polish Wing in 1943/44, and subsequently No 133 Wing in 1944/45.

Unable to return to Poland after the war due to his 'imperialist' parentage, Zumbach resumed Swiss citizenship. Rather then settling down, he became a smuggler, shipping 'cargoes' ranging from wrist watches (to Britain) to arms and soldiers (to Israel). In the mid-1950s he opened a restaurant and night-club in Paris, but eventually returned to his 'old way's in the early 1960s when he organised the Katangese Air Force following a request by the country's dictator, Moise Tshombe – five years later 'Mr John Brown' (the *nom de guerre* adopted by Zumbach during his mercenary days) got involved in another similarly ill-fated affair in Biafra. He then returned to Europe and settled down in France. Following his death in 1986, Jan Zumbach was buried in Warsaw.

APPENDICES

PAF PERSONNEL RANKS

Polish Air Force (PAF) ranks were identical to those of the army. Flying personnel were identified by adding the word *pilot* (abbreviated pil.) or *obserwator* (*obs.*) after the rank for pilots and navigators respectively. In order to keep things simple, the pil. suffixes are omitted in this book, although every fighter pilot's rank had it. In the PAF one had to be a commissioned officer to become an 'observer' (navigator), although even a private could become a pilot. Indeed, some of the aces mentioned in this book scored their first kills with just such a modest rank.

Although Polish airmen in France in 1940 used unchanged an PAF rank system, things got complicated when they arrived in Britain. Polish personnel in effect had two parallel ranks – Polish and British. In this book either Polish or RAF ranks are quoted (official documents typically used only one of these), and it must be kept firmly in mind that these were not equivalent! Pilots with the rank of *szeregowy* up to *plutonowy* were grouped together as RAF sergeants, as were Polish NCOs with the rank of *sierżant*. At higher levels too, Polish ranks were often lower to their RAF equivalent. For example, when in September 1940 Witold Urbanowicz assumed command of No 303 Sqn, and thus becoming a squadron leader, his PAF rank remained as *porucznik* – or precisely *porucznik pilot obserwator* (*por. pil. obs.*), as he had completed officers' training in both areas.

rank	abbreviation	translation	RAF equivalent
szeregowy	szer.	private	aircraftsman
starszy szeregowy	st. szer.	senior private	leading aircraftsman
kapral	kpr.	corporal	senior aircraftsman
plutonowy	plut.	platoon commander	corporal
sierżant	sierż.	sergeant	sergeant
starszy sierżant	st. sierż.	senior sergeant	flight sergeant
chorąży	chor.	warrant officer	warrant officer
podporucznik	ppor.	sub-lieutenant	pilot officer
porucznik	por.	lieutenant	flying officer
kapitan	kpt.	captain	flight lieutenant
major	mjr	major	squadron leader
podpułkownik	ppłk	sub-colonel	wing commander
pułkownik	płk	colonel	group captain
generał brygady	gen. bryg.	brigadier general	air commodore
generał dywizji	gen. dyw.	divisional general	air vice marshal
generał broni (generał lotnictwa)	gen. broni (gen. lotn.)	army general (air force general)	air marshal
generał armii	gen. armii	army general	Air Chief Marshal

Fighter units of the Polish Air Force - Order of Battle

1 August 1939

***1 Pułk Lotniczy* – Warsaw**
Zgrupowanie Mysliwskie
III/1 Dywizjon – Warsaw-Okęcie
111 Eskadra Kościuszkowska
112 Eskadra
IV/1 Dywizjon – Warsaw-Okęcie
113 Eskadra
114 Eskadra

***2 Pułk Lotniczy* – Cracow**
III/2 Dywizjon – Cracow-Rakowice
121 Eskadra
122 Eskadra
123 Eskadra

***3 Pułk Lotniczy* – Poznań**
III/3 Dywizjon – Poznań-Ławica
131 Eskadra
132 Eskadra

***4 Pułk Lotniczy* – Toruń**
III/4 Dywizjon – Toruń
141 Eskadra
142 Eskadra

***5 Pułk Lotniczy* – Lida** (now in Belarus)
III/5 Dywizjon – Wilno (now Vilnius in Lithuania)
151 Eskadra
152 Eskadra

***6 Pułk Lotniczy* – Lwów** (now Lviv in Ukraine)
III/6 Dywizjon – Lwów-Porubanek
161 Eskadra
162 Eskadra

1 September 1939

AIR DEFENCE

***Brygada Pościgowa* – Warsaw area**

III/1 Dywizjon – Zielonka (5 km north-east of Warsaw)
111 Eskadra Kościuszkowska (P.11)
112 Eskadra (P.11)

IV/1 Dywizjon – Poniatów (11 km north of Warsaw)
113 Eskadra (P.11)
114 Eskadra (P.11)
123 Eskadra (P.7)

Centrum Wyszkolenia Lotnictwa nr 1 defence section
(3 P.11 aircraft from *3 Pułk Lotniczy*) – Dęblin

ARMY AVIATION

***Kraków* Army**
121 Eskadra (P.11) – Balice (12 km west of Cracow)
1 section (4 a/c) readiness at Aleksandrowice (Bielsko-Biała)
122 Eskadra (P.11) – Balice

***Poznań* Army**
131 Eskadra (P.11) – Dzierżnica (16 km south-east of Poznań)
1 section (3 a/c) readiness at Poznań
132 Eskadra (P.11) – Dzierżnica

***Pomorze* Army**
141 Eskadra (P.11) – Markowo (22 km south west of Toruń)
142 Eskadra (P.11) – Markowo
1 section (3 a/c) readiness at Toruń

***Modlin* Army**
152 Eskadra (P.11) – Szpandowo (50 km north-west of Warsaw)

***Łódź* Army**
161 Eskadra (P.11) – Widzew (3 km east of Łódź)
162 Eskadra (P.7) – Widzew

***Narew* Independent Operational Group**
151 Eskadra (P.7) – Biel (80 km north-east of Warsaw)

Polish Fighter Aces

It has been assumed for this volume that the definition of an ace is any pilot who participated in the destruction of at least five enemy aircraft. Shared victories were identified as such, rather than being converted to fractions and summed up. This principle was used by Christopher Shores and Clive Williams in their book *Aces High* (1994 edition), which forms the foundation for any further research on the subject of RAF (and, in fact, other air forces') fighter aces of World War 2. Any attempt to verify all victory credits would go far beyond the scope of this book, so the authors therefore accepted the information of the Polish Liaison Officer to HQ Fighter Command, included in the report *Polish Fighter Pilots Achievements During the Second World War (1.9.1939 - 6.5.1945)* [No. FC/S.5/1/AIR/CPLO.INTEL], dated 25 March 1946 (referred to hereinafter as Report). In the few cases where the figures of the Report were amended, the official figures are given in square brackets and comments added below to explain.

Pilot's				score (individual + shared)		
RAF number	last rank	name		confirmed	probable	damaged
P.2095	Flg Off	Mieczysław	Adamek	5+2	1	0
P.794457	Wt Off	Jakub	Bargiełowski	5	0	3
P.1901	Plt Off	Marian	Bełc	7	0	0
P.1681	Flt Lt	Stanisław	Blok	5	1	3
P.1902	Flt Lt	Stanisław	Brzeski	7+3	2	1
P.1300	Flt Lt	Stanisław	Chałupa	3+2	2	0
P.783023	Wt Off	Aleksander	Chudek	9	1	1
P.1902	Flt Lt	Michał	Cwynar	5+1	1	0
P.76731	Sqn Ldr	Bolesław	Drobiński	7	1+1	0
P.0493	Wg Cdr	Jan	Falkowski	9	1	0
P.1387	Flt Lt	Mirosław	Ferić	8+2	1	1
P.0163	Grp Capt	Aleksander	Gabszewicz	8+3	1+1	3
P.1392	Flt Lt	Bolesław	Gładych[1]	17 [14]	2	0+1
P.1527	Sqn Ldr	Antoni	Głowacki	8+1	3	4
P.1495	Flt Lt	Czesław	Główczyński	5+1	2	1
P.1298	Sqn Ldr	Władysław	Gnyś	2+3	0	1
P.1393	Sqn Ldr	Zdzisław	Henneberg	8+2	1	1
P.0273	Sqn Ldr	Eugeniusz	Horbaczewski	16+1	1	1
P.0700	Wg Cdr	Stefan	Janus	6	0	1
P.1654	Sqn Ldr	Józef	Jeka	7+1	0	3
P.793420	Sgt	Stanisław	Karubin	7	0	0
P.0696	Sqn Ldr	Tadeusz	Koc	3+3	3	0
P.0296	Flt Lt	Kazimierz	Kosiński	2+3	2	0+2
P.1400	*Wg Cdr*	*Julian*	*Kowalski*[2]	*3+1 [4+1]*	*4*	*1 [2]*
P.1531	Plt Off	Jan	Kremski	3+6	0+1	0+4
P.1299	Wg Cdr	Wacław	Król	8+1	1	0+1
P.1506	Sqn Ldr	Wacław	Łapkowski	6+1	0	1
P.1492	Sqn Ldr	Witold	Łokuciewski	8	3+1	0
P.1912	Plt Off	Michał	Maciejowski[3]	10+1 [9+1]	1	1
P.1288	Wg Cdr	Mieczysław	Mümler	5+1	0	1+1
P.76704	Flg Off	Tadeusz	Nowak	4+1	1	1
P.1913	Flt Lt	Eugeniusz	Nowakiewicz	4+2	1	0+1
P.76803	Grp Capt	Tadeusz	Nowierski[4]	4+1 [3]	1	5 [6+1]
P.0042	Flg Off	Ludwik	Paszkiewicz	6	0	0
P.2093	Flt Lt	Adolf	Pietrasiak	7+4	0	0+2
P.1915	Sqn Ldr	Henryk	Pietrzak	7+1	1	1
P.1381	Wg Cdr	Marian	Pisarek	11+2	1	2
P.76707	Sqn Ldr	Karol	Pniak	6+2	2	2+2
P.782474	Wt Off	Mieczysław	Popek	3+3	0	2
P.76751	Sqn Ldr	Jerzy	Popławski	5	0	2
P.1856	Sqn Ldr	Władysław	Potocki	4+2	0	1
P.1427	Sqn Ldr	Jerzy	Radomski	2+3	0+1	4
P.0692	Wg Cdr	Kazimierz	Rutkowski	5+1	2	1
P.76710	Wg Cdr	Stanisław	Skalski	18+3	2	4+1
P.1624	Flt Lt	Grzegorz	Sołogub	5	1	0
P.54304	Maj	Wacław	Sobański[5]	4+1 [-]	1 [-]	4 [-]
P.0448	Flt Lt	Kazimierz	Sporny	5	1	1

Pilot's RAF no.	last rank	name		score (individual + shared) confirmed	probable	damaged
P.76713	Flg Off	Franciszek	Surma	5	3+1	1
P.1653	Flt Lt	Eugeniusz	Szaposznikow	8+1	0	1
P.76781	Sqn Ldr	Henryk	Szczęsny	8+3	1	2
P.782842	Wt Off	Kazimierz	Sztramko	4+1	0	0
P.76735	Grp Capt	Witold	Urbanowicz[6]	18 [17]	1	0
P.0603	Sqn Ldr	Marian	Wesołowski	2+4	0	1+4
P.76730	Grp Capt	Stefan	Witorzeńć	5+1	0	2
P.76736	Flg Off	Bolesław	Własnowolski	5+1	0	0
P.781062	Wt Off	Mirosław	Wojciechowski	4+1	0	0
P.2096	Flt Lt	Kazimierz	Wünsche	4+1	1	0
P.1382	Wg Cdr	Jan	Zumbach	12+1	5	1

Footnotes

1. The 14 kills credited to Gładych in the Report did not include three German aircraft destroyed in 1944 whilst flying with the USAAF. One of these was erroneously categorised by the PAF as 'destroyed on the ground', while two others (confirmed by USAAF authorities) were achieved when Gładych was no longer in service with the PAF.

2. There is no evidence for one kill and one damaged, credited in the Report. It seems that the score of Flt Lt Jan Kowalski (P.1909, one destroyed, one damaged) was erroneously added due to the similarity of the names.

3. It is believed that an aerial kill achieved when flying with No 249 Sqn, RAF, was erroneously categorised by the PAF as 'destroyed on the ground'.

4. British documents as late as mid-1941 credited Nowierski with five German aircraft destroyed and two shared destroyed (plus probables and damaged) while flying Spitfires with No 609 Sqn between August 1940 and February 1941. The score was downgraded in the Report to 3 destroyed, 1 probable and $6\frac{1}{2}$ damaged. However, identities of at least five German aircraft downed by Nowierski during that period (including one shared) have been traced by historians so far.

5. As Sobański never flew with the PAF, his score was not included in the Report. The figures here were taken from the 4th FG scoreboard.

6. Contrary to some accounts, the Report figure included the Japanese fighters Urbanowicz destroyed, but (obviously) omitted the Soviet aircraft he downed in 1936.

Following the pattern of *Aces High*, the list of Polish pilots credited with four enemy aircraft destroyed is given below

Pilot's RAF no.	last rank	name		confirmed	probable	damaged
P.1290	Sqn Ldr	Tadeusz	Czerwi ski	4	0	0
P.0213	Flt Lt	Władysław	Drecki[1]	4 [3]	0	1
-	por.	Hieronim	Dudwał	4	0	0
P.784079	Wt Off	Ryszard	Idrian[2]	4 [2]	0	0
P.1385	Flg Off	Wojciech	Januszewicz[3]	4 [3]	0	0
P.0711	Flt Lt	Witold	Łanowski[4]	4 [2]	0	0
P.0248	Sqn Ldr	Witold	Retinger[5]	4	0	2
P.76762	Plt Off	Władysław	Różycki	4	0	2
P.2094	Flt Lt	Michał	Turżański	4	0	0
P.1808	Flt Lt	Janusz	Walawski	4	0	3
P.1291	Flt Lt	Stefan	Wapniarek	4	0	0

Footnotes

1. Drecki scored his final kill in a British-manned squadron in the Mediterranean, two days before he was killed in an accident. Consequently, his report was never submitted to the Polish Air Force, and this victory (confirmed by appropriate RAF authorities) was not included in the Report. There are also unconfirmed accounts of yet another kill he scored, but was not credited with.

2. On 7 December 1944 Wt Off Idrian claimed two Fw 190s destroyed off the Norwegian coast. This claim was not credited because the Focke-Wulfs collided without him firing a shot. However, another Polish pilot was officially credited with the destruction of enemy aircraft in a virtually identical case, so Wt Off Idrian is included here.

3. Januszewicz is officially credited with three kills between 3 and 6 September 1939. It is now believed that he scored a fourth confirmed victory during that period as well. As he was killed early in the Battle of Britain, he was not able to submit the claims himself when the Report was prepared (the original documents being destroyed in 1939).

4. Łanowski claimed all his victories with the USAAF. The Report credited him with only two kills, as he scored the remaining two (confirmed by USAAF authorities) when no longer in PAF service.

5. Retinger claimed five kills, but one of those was later downgraded to a damaged.

There were no aces among Polish nightfighter pilots, and the three top scoring night flyers are listed below

P.2094	Flt Lt	Michał	Turżanski	4	0	0
P.0663	Sqn Ldr	Gerard	Ranoszek	3	0	2
P.1404	Sqn Ldr	Antoni	Alexandrowicz	3	0	0

Finally, several Allied aces scored kills flying with Polish units. The listing below quotes their scores and highest ranks whilst with PAF. Their eventual scores are given in square brackets

pilot's nationality	RAF number	rank	name		score (individual+shared) confirmed	probable	damaged
British	40667	Wg Cdr	John Robert	Braham[1]	3 [29]	0 [2]	0 [5]
British	37499	Flt Lt	Athol Stanhope	Forbes	7 [7+2]	1 [1]	0 [0]
Czech	793451	Sgt	Josef	Frantisek	17 [17]	1 [1]	0 [0]
British	90082	Sqn Ldr	Ronald Gustave	Kellett	5 [5]	2 [2]	1 [1]
Canadian	37106	Wg Cdr	John Alexander	Kent	7 [12]	2 [3]	1 [3]
British (Irish)	37422	Flt Lt	William	Riley	2 [8+2]	2 [3]	0 [1]
British	29048	Sqn Ldr	William Arthur	Satchell	3 [7]	3 [5]	0 [12+1]
Soviet		por.	Viktor	Kalinovski	2 [12]	-	-

Footnote

1. Braham never actually served with a Polish unit, but scored three kills in Mosquito FB VIs borrowed from No 305 (Polish) Bomber Squadron.

Polish V1 Aces

Polish pilots who participated in destruction of at least five V1 flying bombs

pilot's RAF number	rank	name		*V1s* individual + shared	summarised total	*enemy aircraft* confirmed	probable	damaged
P.783248	Wt Off	C	Bartłomiejczyk	5	5	1	-	-
P.1595	Flt Lt	Antoni	Cholajda	5+1	51/2	2	1	2
P.1902	Flt Lt	Michal	Cwynar	1+4	3	5+1	1	-
P.0273	Sqn Ldr	Eugeniusz	Horbaczewski	1+4	3	16+1	1	1
P.780386	Flt Sgt	Tadeusz	Jankowski	4+4	6	2+1	-	1
P.0973	Flg Off	Stefan	Karnkowski	2+3	$3^{1}/2$	1+1	1	-
P.0387	Flt Lt	Włodzimierz	Klawe	2+4	$3^{2}/3$	1+1	2	-
P.0327	Flt Lt	Longin	Majewski	5+1	$5^{1}/2$	0+1	-	-
P.2913	Sgt	Jerzy Andrzej	Mielnicki	6	6	-	-	-
P.783147	Wt Off	Aleksander	Pietrzak	4+1	$4^{1}/4$	3+1	-	2
P.1915	Flt Lt	Henryk	Pietrzak	4+1	$4^{1}/2$	7+1	1	1
P.780965	Wt Off	Jan	Rogowski	3+2	4	2	-	-
P.782513	Flt Sgt	S	Rudowski	7+3	$8^{1}/2$	2	-	1
P.1032	Flt Lt	Jan	Siekierski	7+3	$8^{1}/6$	1	-	1
P.783226	Flt Sgt	Kazimierz	Siwek	2+3	$3^{1}/12$	3	-	-
P.0744	Flt Lt	Teofil	Szymankiewicz	5+1	$5^{1}/2$	0+1	-	-
P.781044	Wt Off	Tadeusz	Szymanski	8	8	2	1	-
P.2478	Flg Off	Gwido	Swistun	1+5	$3^{1}/2$	2+1	1	-
-	Flt Sgt	Józef	Zaleński	5+6	8	-	-	-

The following fighter aces scored less than five V1s

Flt Lt	Stanisław	Blok	1
Sqn Ldr	Józef	Jeka	1
Grp Capt	Tadeusz	Nowierski	1
Wt Off	Jakub	Bargiełowski	3

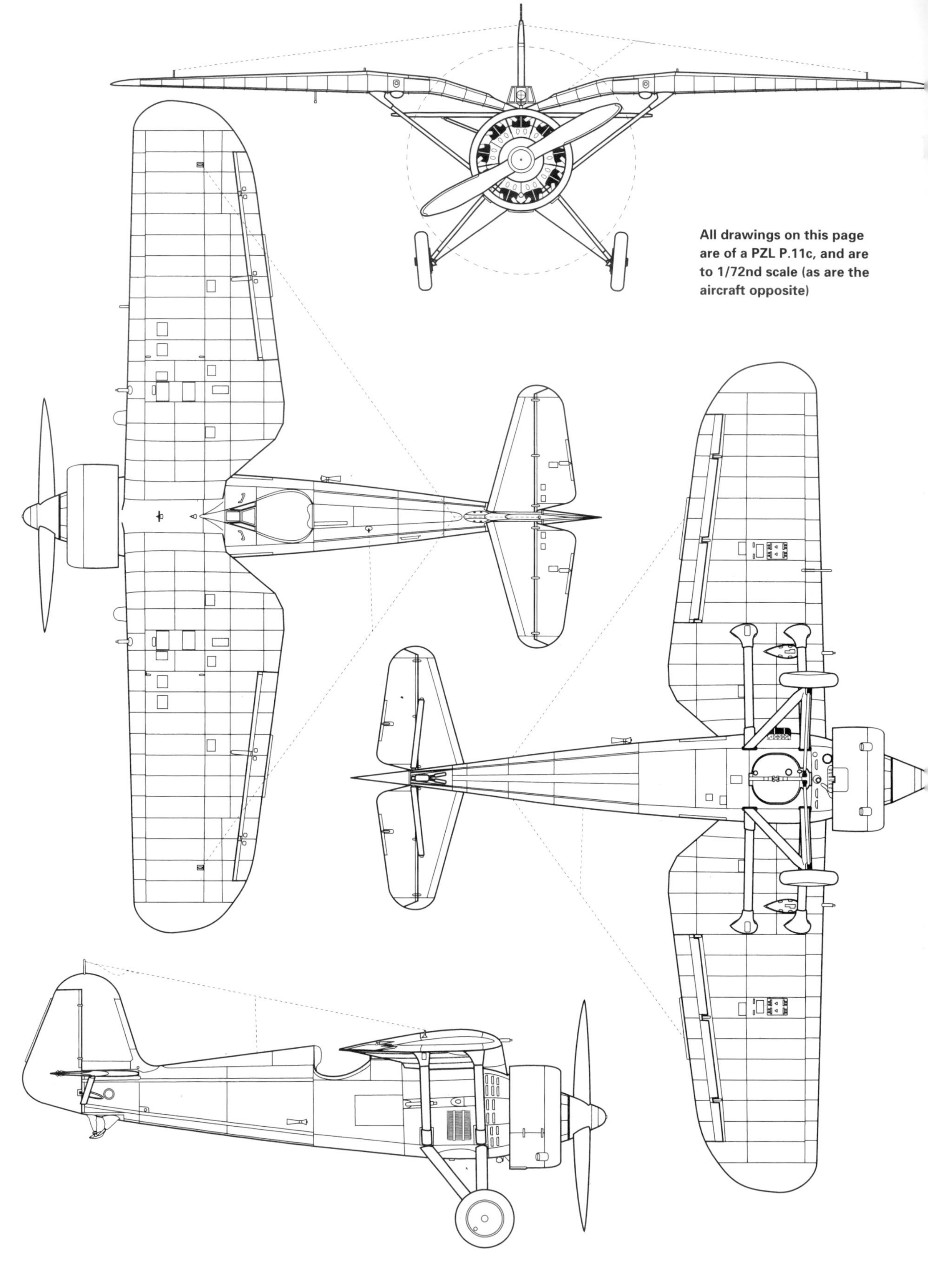

All drawings on this page are of a PZL P.11c, and are to 1/72nd scale (as are the aircraft opposite)

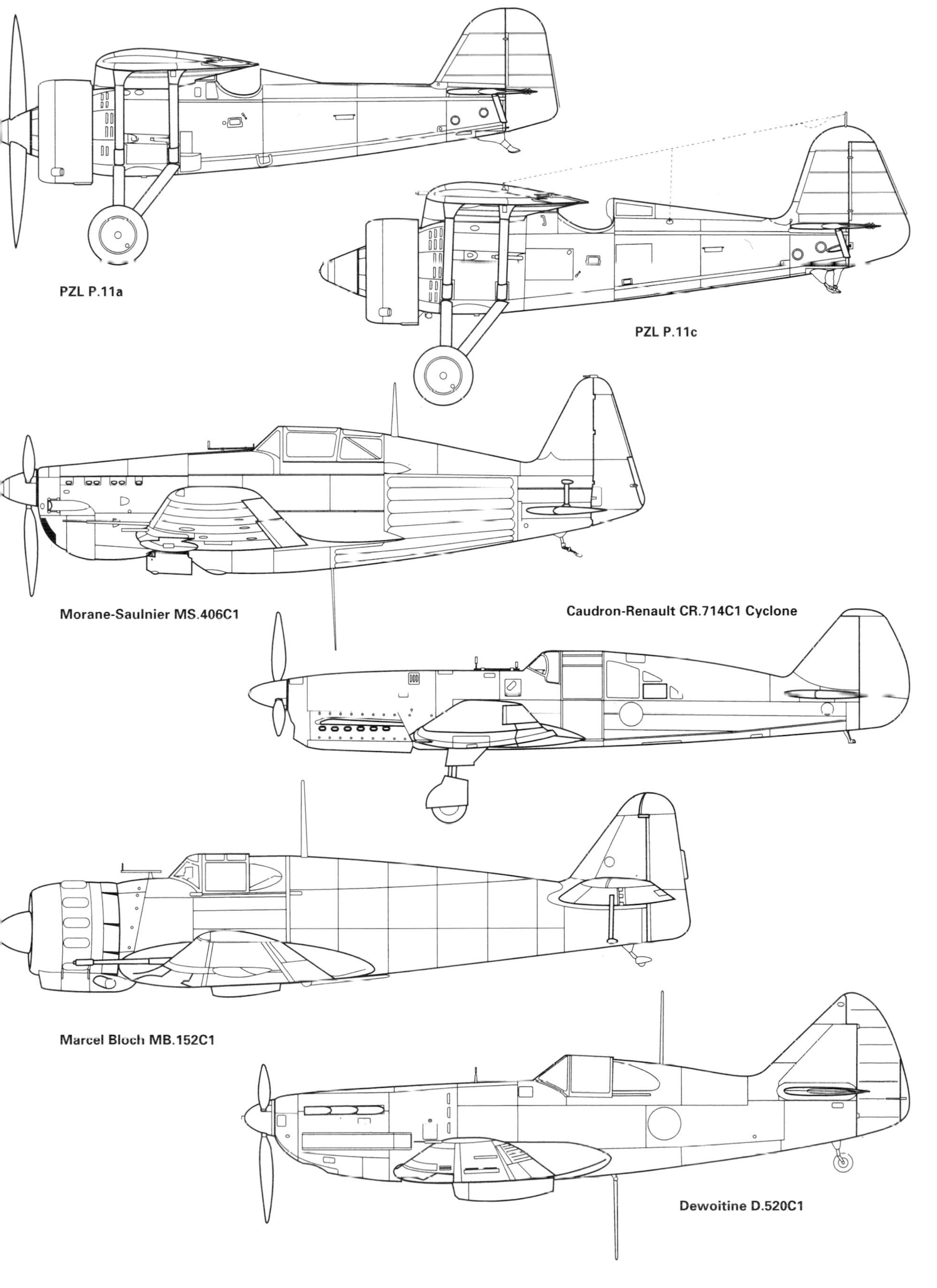
PZL P.11a
PZL P.11c
Morane-Saulnier MS.406C1
Caudron-Renault CR.714C1 Cyclone
Marcel Bloch MB.152C1
Dewoitine D.520C1

Colour Plates

1

P.11c 8.70 'White 10' of ppor. Hieronim Dudwał, *113 Eskadra*, Poniatów, September 1939

Badly shot up on 1 September whilst reputedly being flown by ppor. Dudwał, 'White 10' was repaired by simply rivetting two bare metal sheets both along and across the fuselage. Dudwał also opened his score on this date, whilst his fourth victim (a Hs 126 downed on 16 September) was the last Luftwaffe aircraft claimed by a PAF fighter pilot in 1939.

2

P.11c 8.110 'White 4' of kpr. Stanisław Brzeski, *152 Eskadra*, Szpandowo, September 1939

Brzeski was downed by flak in this P.11c on 4 September when attacking a German balloon – he had already destroyed one the day before, thus probably becoming the only World War 2 ace to claim the destruction of an enemy observation balloon as part of his score. Brzeski scored his first heavier-than-air kill (a Bf 109) in February 1941 whilst part of No 249 Sqn. He subsequently scored five and one shared kills with No 317 Sqn, before moving to No 302 Sqn in 1943, where he claimed one shared and two probables. In May 1944, while part of No 303 Sqn, he was shot down and made a PoW.

3

P.11c 8.63 'White 2' of ppor. Wacław Król, *121 Eskadra*, Podlodów, September 1939

Boasting stripes across the fuselage and an 'arrowhead' of two wider stripes in the same colour on top of the wing, this P.11c was marked up as the unit commander's aircraft – this scheme is presently worn by the world's only surviving P.11c, which is on display at the Polish Aviation Museum in Cracow. Król claimed his first kill on 5 September 1939 when he shared in the destruction of a Do 17 near Dęblin. He subsequently became the only Polish pilot to be credited with kills in four different theatres – Poland, France, Britain and Africa.

4

MS.406C1 936 'White III' of ppor. Władysław Gnyś, GC III/1, Moerbecke, May 1940

For about a week in mid-May GC III/1 was based at Moerbecke, near Ghent, in Belgium. During this time Gnyś was credited with three bombers shared destroyed to thus become the PAF's second ace. He later flew with the RAF.

5

CR.714 Cyclone I-234 'White 2' of ppor. Czesław Główczyński, GC I/145, Villacoublay, May 1940

On 9 June 1940 Główczyński scored his fifth kill of the war (a Bf 109), plus a second as a probable. Although his CR.714 was damaged in the combat, it was hastily repaired, and he was able to scramble in the afternoon and also claim a Do 17 probably destroyed. Główczyński would later get a kill with No 302 Sqn in Britain.

6

D.520C1 119 of ppłk Mieczysław Mümler, GC II/7, Luxeuil, June 1940

Wearing typical Battle of France markings, this Dewoitine carried no distinguishing unit colours or motifs, being identifiable only by its factory number on the rudder. Mümler was flying this aeroplane on 15 June 1940 when he was credited with a Do 17 shared destroyed and a He 111 shared damaged.

7

MB.151C1 57 of por. Zdzisław Henneberg, *Escadrille de Chasse et de Defence He*, Chateauroux, June 1940

The 'Chimney Flight' in defence of the Bloch assembly plant at Chateauroux was code-named *He*, which was short for Henneberg. On 5 June the flight's namesake downed a He 111 for his first victory, and 13 days later he flew an MB.152 to Tangmere – Henneberg scored eight kills with No 303 Sqn during the Battle of Britain. Appointed the unit's OC, he was lost on 12 April 1941 when Air-Sea Rescue (ASR) failed to locate him after he had ditched his Spitfire into the Channel.

8

Hurricane I P3208 of Sgt Antoni Głowacki, No 501 Sqn, Gravesend, August 1940

Aside from being flown by Sgt Głowacki, P3208 was also used by fellow Pole Plt Off Paweł Zenker (two kills in August 1940). On 18 August the Hurricane was downed by Oberleutnant Gerhard Schöpfel of JG 26, its pilot, Plt Off J W Bland, being killed in the action. Głowacki claimed eight victories during the Battle of Britain (including five on 28 August), making him one of the most succesful Polish pilots of the campaign.

9

Hurricane I V7235 of Flg Off Ludwik Paszkiewicz, No 303 Sqn, Northolt, August 1940

RF-M was Flg Off Paszkiewicz's favourite Hurricane, for he used it to shoot down two Do 17Zs on 7 September, a Bf 110 four days later, a Bf 109 on the 15th and a He 111 on the 26th – the following day 'Paszko' met his death in L1696/RF-T. V7235's subsequent pilots included Sgt Bełc, who shot down a Bf 110 on 5 October. Amazingly, by December 1940 this Hurricane was the only survivor of the original complement of Hawker fighters issued to the squadron in August .

10

Hurricane I V6605 of Plt Off Zdzisław Henneberg, No 303 Sqn, Northolt, 7 September 1940

At the opposite end of the longevity scale from V7235, this Hurricane was used by No 303 Sqn for just a matter of a few hours on 7 September. In its first week of operations, the Polish unit amazed previously sceptical RAF officials with its successes. However, these came at a price in machinery (if not personnel), which is why on 7 September Plt Off Henneberg had to borrow V6605 from No 1 Sqn, RCAF, (also based at Northolt) in order to lead 'A' Flight into combat. Flying the 'Canadian' Hurricane, 'Dzidek' Henneberg claimed a Bf 109 destroyed and a probable, before returning the borrowed aeroplane to its owners' ever so slightly damaged.

11

Hurricane I P3939 of Sqn Ldr Witold Urbanowicz, OC No 303 Sqn, Northolt, September 1940

After the hard fighting of 6/7 September, No 303 Sqn faced a shortage of aircraft – P3939 was duly acquired on 8 September from No 302 Sqn, the aircraft having previously been coded WX-H and flown by (among others) Plt Off Julian 'Roch' Kowalski, the unit's top-scoring pilot during the Battle. Whilst in service with No 303 Sqn, the Hurricane retained the Polish square beneath the canopy. Although P3939 was principally flown by Witold Urbanowicz, it was also used by Plt Off Zumbach. Finally, on 15 September Sgt Tadeusz Andruszków used the Hurricane to claim a share in the destruction of a Do 17Z with Sgt Wojciechowski. Three hours later P3939 was shot up by Unteroffizier Heinrich Kopperschager of 1./JG 53, forcing Andruszków to bale out south of Dartford.

12

Hurricane I V6684 of Sqn Ldr Witold Urbanowicz, OC No 303 Sqn, Northolt, September 1940

Urbanowicz was flying V6684 on 15 September when he downed two Do 17Zs of 8./KG 2 (Wk-Nr 2549/U5+FS and Wk-Nr 4245/U5+GS). On 26 and 27 September Flg Off Zumbach claimed two Bf 109s and a He 111 with it, then on the afternoon of the 27th Flt Lt Kent destroyed a 5./KG 77 Ju 88A-1 (Wk-Nr 7106/3Z+GN) over the Sussex coast. Further success came V6684's way on 5 October when Flg Off Henneberg was credited with a Bf 110. The Hurricane was also flown by numerous other PAF aces, including Plt Off Ferić and Sgt Wünsche, as well as Sqn Ldr Kellett. At the end of the Battle of Britain a cartoon caricature of Adolf Hitler and the final No 303 Sqn score were chalked onto the aircraft's fuselage.

13

Hurricane I V7504 of Sgt Stanisław Karubin, No 303 Sqn, Northolt, September 1940

Karubin downed 4./JG 53's Unteroffizier Karl Vogl in Bf 109E-1 (Wk-Nr 6384) off Beachy Head whilst flying V7504 on 30 September. No 303 Sqn OC Sqn Ldr Kellett also used it to damage a Bf 109 over Rochester on 5 October. Karubin claimed six aircraft with No 303 Sqn, having previously flown with *111 Eskadra* in 1939 (destroying a Bf 110) and the MB.152-equipped ECD I/55 in France. After leaving No 303 Sqn, he was posted firstly to No 58 OTU and then No 55 OTU, where he was killed in Hurricane I V7742 on 12 October 1941.

14

Hurricane II Z2405 of Flt Lt Aleksander Gabszewicz, No 316 Sqn, Church Stanton, summer 1941

Prior to its service with No 316 Sqn, this Hurricane had been used by No 56 Sqn for camouflage testing – hence the odd roundel style and grey-green livery (at that time Dark Earth-Dark Green still reigned supreme in Fighter Command). Gabszewicz flew Z2405 as 'B' Flight commander until No 316 Sqn re-equipped with Spitfires in the autumn 1941. Prior to a unit badge being officially adopted in early 1942, both *113* and *114 Eskadra* emblems were applied to No 316 Sqn's aircraft – Gabszewicz came from *114 Eskadra*, so his Hurricane was adorned with a swallow. By 1941 he had been credited with a shared kill over Warsaw, a He 111 over Lyon on 1 June 1940 and two shared kills in Hurricanes with No 316 Sqn.

15

Hurricane II Z3675 of Plt Off Kazimierz Sporny, No 302 Sqn, Church Stanton, September 1941

Sporny was flying Z3675 on 4 September when he was credited with a Bf 109 probably destroyed in his first successful encounter with the enemy. This Hurricane was one of sixteen ferried by No 302 Sqn to Lichfield on 10 October 1941, these aircraft then being promptly crated up and sent to the USSR. Interestingly, Z3675 was later used in a training establishment at Sverdlovsk whilst still wearing full No 302 Sqn markings! Sporny got his first kill in late 1941, with most of his successes coming later with 'Skalski's Circus' in 1943.

16

Spitfire I L1082 of Flg Off Tadeusz 'Novi' Nowierski, No 609 Sqn, Warmwell, 13 August 1940

13 August was Nowierski's first day of operations with No 609 Sqn, the unit intercepting a formation of II./StG 2 Ju 87s during the afternoon. 'Novi', as part of Flt Lt McArthur's 'Green' section, engaged the Stukas' escorts, and was duly credited with a Bf 109 destroyed and another damaged. His victim, Bf 109E-1 'Black 9' of 5./JG 53, crashed into Weymouth Bay, its pilot, Feldwebel Hans-Heinz Pfannschmidt baling out to become a PoW. L1082 was written off 11 days whilst being flown by American Plt Off Mamedoff.

17

Spitfire II P8079 of Flt Lt Wacław Łapkowski, No 303 Sqn, Northolt, March 1941

When delivered to Fighter Command from the factory, P8079 lacked the recently-adopted Sky fuselage band, so this had to be carefully applied (so as not to obliterate the serial) at No 37 MU, at Burtonwood, in February 1941. Sadly, once the fighter got to No 303 Sqn, the skill of the latter unit's riggers hardly matched that of their MU brethren, and the RF codes fairly obliterated much of the serial! Although P8079 was usually Flt Lt Łapkowski's mount, during March and April 1941 it was occasionally used by other pilots, including aces Sqn Ldr Henneberg (OC No 303 Sqn), Plt off Łokuciewski and Sgt Bełc. On 20 April Sgt Jan Palak achieved P8079's only combat success when he damaged a Ju 88. In early May the aircraft left No 303 Sqn and passed through a number of RAF establishments before finally reaching No 61 OTU. On 27 April 1944 Pole Sgt Eugeniusz Jaworski was flying P8079 when it collided with another Spitfire, killing both pilots.

18

Spitfire II P8385 *IMPREGNABLE* of Flg Off Mirosław 'Ox' Ferić, No 303 Sqn, Northolt, May-July 1941

Between 15 May and 12 July 1941 P8385 was Ferić's personal mount. On 22 June, at 1610, he claimed a Bf 109E destroyed, followed five days later at 1215 by a Bf 109F damaged. P8385's other squadron pilots included Plt Offs Gładych and Drecki, Sgts Popek and Jan Szlagowski (who used it to probably destroy a Bf 109F on 23 June), Flt Lt Tadeusz Arentowicz (claimed a Bf 109 damaged with it on 25 June) and Flg Off Zumbach (one Bf 109E destroyed and another as a probable on 2 July, again with P8385). In mid-July 1941 the Spitfire was transferred to No 306 Sqn. Mirosław Ferić, who claimed seven German aircraft destroyed during the Battle of Britain, was killed in a flying accident on 14 February 1942.

19

Spitfire II P7855 *KRYSIA* of Flg Off Jan 'Kon' Falkowski, No 315 Sqn, Northolt, July/August 1941

Already a veteran of two frontline tours (hence the heavily worn No 65 'East India' Sqn titling beneath the cockpit), P7855 also had a rather odd Sky fuselage band, applied at No 24 MU, which was aligned with the number 19 fuselage frame – hence the slope! The oversize Polish square on the cowling was typical of the marking applied by No 308 Sqn, from whom P7855 was 'acquired' (like most of No 315 Sqn's Mk IIs). The marking was painted level on the ground, which explains its skewed appearance when in flight. Following true No 315 Sqn fashion, the aircraft letter was turned into a girl's name (Krysia, or Christine in English). P7855 was repeatedly flown by Flg Off Falkowski, who was known to friends as 'Koń' (Horse). Having scored one kill up to mid-1941, he had taken his score to seven by October. In 1943 Falkowski, took command of No 303 Sqn, and would eventually become OC 3rd Polish Fighter Wing by war's end.

20

Spitfire II P8387 *HALINA/BARTY* of Sgt Stanisław 'Charlie' Blok, No 315 Sqn, Northolt, August 1941

Continuing No 315 Sqn's tradition of giving its aircraft female names, P8387 was called *HALINA* – it also boasted an oversize Polish square (denoting its previous service with No 308 Sqn). The presentation name *BARTY* was also worn just forward of the cockpit. Note that the aircraft's serial has been reapplied just behind the Sky band at No 9 MU, following the addition of the new recognition marking. *HALINA* was regularly flown by Blok, who was then known only for his seaman's parentage and stubborn character. He would open his score during the summer of 1941, claiming two Bf 109s.

21

Spitfire V AB824 of Sgt Marian Bełc, No 303 Sqn, Northolt, October 1941

Sgt Bełc flew this Spitfire on 24 October 1941 when he claimed his seventh confirmed kill (a Bf 109E) between Calais and Cap Gris Nez at 1510. AB824 was lost on 4 April 1942 whilst being flown by Flt Lt Zbigniew Kustrzyński who, being bored with his Ops Room posting, had joined his parent squadron on a mission. Attacked near St Omer, he claimed two Fw 190s before his Spitfire was hit. With a glycol leak and no chance of getting back to Britain, Kustrzyński force-landed in France. AB824 was recovered and apparently later used by the Germans.Note the aircraft's non-standard letter S and the Sky band applied parallel to the inclined frame.

22

Spitfire V W3506/RF-U *HENDON LAMB* of Sgt Mieczysław Adamek, No 303 Sqn, Northolt, December 1941

Adamek was flying W3506 as wingman to Flg Off Gładych when, on 8 December 1941, No 303 Sqn led the Northolt Wing on a sweep over the Le Touquet area. On the way back the wing was bounced by Germans, and Plt Off Groszewski of No 315 Sqn baled out – Gładych circled the lone dinghy, pinpointing it for the ASR. When he was subsequently attacked by an Fw 190, Sgt Adamek shot the fighter down into the Channel. Sadly, despite their efforts Groszewski was never found. On 12 April 1942 it was the turn of W3506 to be shot down into the Channel, with Sgt Wojda baling out. He had more luck, however, and was picked by a rescue launch. Note the absence of the PAF insignia on this aircraft, and how the unit badge was applied close to the presentation emblem. As the badge was always located in the same place, some aircraft actually had it applied over the presentation name!

23

Spitfire V P8742 *Ada* of Flg Off Czesław Główczyński, No 302 Sqn, Harrowbeer, December 1941

Delivered to No 302 Sqn on 5 December, this aircraft had been damaged by mid-month. Repaired, it served with the unit through to April 1942, after which time it saw service with several RAF units until written off in a take-off accident at Perranporth whilst with No 317 Sqn in July 1943. Główczyński was already an ace by the time he joined No 302 Sqn at Duxford, and on 17 August 1940 he was seriously wounded in a flying accident in Hurricane P3927/WX-E. He resumed operational flying seven months later (again with No 302 Sqn) and on 30 December 1941 scored his finall kill – a Bf 109F.

24

Spitfire V AD130 of Sqn Ldr Aleksander Gabszewicz, OC No 316 Sqn, Northolt, February 1942

Gabszewicz flew AD130 on several occasions, although it was not his personal mount. On 10 April 1942 Flg Off Józef Dec claimed an Fw 190 probably destroyed whilst flying this fighter, although two days later Flg Off Bernard Buchwald was shot down in it and made a PoW. Apart from the standard markings, including the PAF square with the titling *POLAND* below, the fighter also carried the unit badge behind the cockpit – note also the non-standard shape of the letter Z in the squadron code. Gabszewicz scored three and two shared kills, one and one shared probable and two damaged with No 316 Sqn. He felt so connected with this unit that when appointed wing, and then Sector, OC, he had his personal aircraft coded SZ-G. Flying such a Spitfire, Gabszewicz added a further three kills and a damaged to his score.

25

Spitfire V W3970 of Flg Off Tadeusz Koc, No 317 Sqn, Exeter, early 1942

Koc used W3970 on 8 November 1941 to claim a Bf 109F probably shot down. This Spitfire also proved lucky for him on 15 March 1942 – when No 317 Sqn encountered bad weather, which forced nine Spitfires to crash in dense fog, only Koc, in this Spitfire, and fellow ace Sgt Brzeski (in W3424/JH-Q) managed to land safely. W3970 featured non-standard undersize roundels similar to those found on single-engined night-fighters. This Spitfire was often flown by Plt Offs Janicki and Łanowski, both of whom later flew with the 61st FS/56th FG.

26

Spitfire V EN951/RF-D *Donald Duck* of Sqn Ldr Jan 'Johann' Zumbach, OC No 303 Sqn, Kirton-in-Lindsey, October/November 1942

Originally used by Don Blakeslee of No 133 'Eagle' Sqn to claim several German aircraft over Dieppe on 19 August 1942, EN951 was subsequently issued in late September to Jan Zumbach at No 303 Sqn. Known as 'Johann' because of his Swiss parentage, he was also nicknamed *Donald Duck* (hence the Disney-inspired marking). At that time No 303 Sqn finally introduced the Polish square to its aircraft. Unusually for a PAF unit, EN951 also carried a squadron leader's pennant. Zumbach's scoreboard consisted of 13 black crosses with white outlines, with a small '$^{1}/_{3}$' in white on the last of these (standing for $12^{1}/_{3}$ confirmed kills), four crosses with red outlines (probables) and one without an outline (damaged). The aircraft's serial was applied in small characters at the top of the Sky band. After Zumbach's departure on 1 December, the Spitfire was usually flown by aces Flg Offs Drobiński and Głowacki, or Wt Off Wünsche.

27

Spitfire XII EN222 of Flt Lt Henryk Pietrzak and Flt Lt Władysław Potocki, Intensive Flying Development Flight, High Post, November 1942 to February 1943

Spitfire XIIs EN221 and EN222 were tested at the IFDF from 6 November 1942 until 18 February 1943. Flt Lt (acting) Pietrzak was one of two pilots who commenced these tests, although he was replaced during December by Flt Lt Potocki. One tested feature was the influence of reduced wingspan on aileron response, the aircraft's wingtips being removed and the resulting openings plugged with wooden blocks. It was found that low altitude flight handling and manoeuvrability were improved with shorter span wings, and just such a configuration was adopted for production aircraft. The Mk XII thus became the first clipped-wing Spitfire version to see operational use, as a direct result of the tests carried out by the two Polish aces. Clipped wings were later fitted to many Spitfires, and this could actually be the greatest contribution made by just two Polish Air Force pilots to the RAF's fighter effort.

28

Spitfire IX EN128 of Flg Off Henryk Pietrzak, No 306 Sqn, Northolt, 31 December 1942

This Spitfire exhibits the standard camouflage and markings of the period. The Polish square, with *POLAND* stencilled in capitals beneath it, was painted on the cowling, while the No 306 Sqn badge was applied below the windscreen. Note the lengthy scorch mark (possibly from an engine fire) along the fuselage. EN128 was probably flown by Flg Off Pietrzak on 31 December 1942 when he scored what was subsequently claimed to be the PAF's 500th downed 'Hun'. Before the war Pietrzak had been an NCO with *4 Pułk Lotniczy*, and during the Battle of France he had flown with GC III/9. Commissioned during his service with No 306 Sqn, he later flew Mustangs with No 315 Sqn as 'A' Flight commander. He went on to become the last OC of No 309 Sqn.

29

Spitfire V BM144 *Halszka* of Flg Off Antoni Głowacki, No 303 Sqn, Kirton-in-Lindsey, early 1943

BM144 is well known as the *Donald Duck*-marked RF-D (see *Osprey Aircraft of the Aces 16 - Spitfire Mark V Aces* for further details). When Zumbach changed aircraft, BM144 became RF-H, and served until March 1943 as the mount of Zygmunt Bieńkowski (flight, and then squadron commander). Although RF-H was his personal aeroplane, BM144 was repeatedly flown in early 1943 by ace Flg Off Głowacki. By 1943 BM144 had become an LF VB, with its short wingtip fairings painted Dark Green overall. Like EN951 (and many other Spitfires following an overhaul), its serial has been reapplied in small characters high on the Sky band.

30

Spitfire IX EN267 of Flt Sgt Kazimierz Sztramko, Polish Fighting Team, Goubrine, April 1943

Like virtually every Spitfire IX of the PFT (alias 'C' Flight No 145 Sqn), EN267 featured a digit instead of a code letter. This aeroplane saw considerable action in the African skies, with Sztramko being the most successful of its pilots by claiming an MC 202 and a Bf 109 destroyed on 22 April 1943. Flg Off Horbaczewski flew it on 28 March when he downed a Ju 88 – thus opening the PFT scoreboard. Flg Off Sporny got a Bf 109 on 7 April, and this Spitfire also claimed the last success of the unit when, on 6 May, Sqn Ldr Skalski damaged a Bf 109.

31

Spitfire IX BS463 of Flg Off Michał Mirosław 'Miki' Maciejowski, No 316 Sqn, Northolt, May 1943

BS463 carried the squadron emblem behind the cockpit and a Polish square on the nose. Squadron codes were applied forward of the roundel, stencilled on with distinctive breaks note also that the letter G was larger than the squadron codes. The Spitfire was usually flown by Flg Off Maciejowski, and on 4 May 1943 he used it to probably destroy an Fw 190 and damage a second Focke-Wulf fighter. His score had reached ten and one shared destroyed by June 1943 when he baled out over France and became a PoW. BS463 was also flown by Wg Cdr Gabszewicz and Flt Lts Falkowski and Gnyś.

32

Spitfire IX EN172 of Flg Off Stanisław 'Charlie' Blok, No 315 Sqn, Northolt, May 1943

EN172 was one of the first Mk IXs delivered to No 315 Sqn, where it became the personal mount of Sqn Ldr Sawicz. On 15 May 1943 this Spitfire was flown by Flg Off Blok during 'Circus 297'. He later wrote in his report; 'I noticed 1 F.W. 190 in a slight dive. I attacked him from astern and above from 600 yds. I clearly saw flashes on him, and he took no evasive action. I followed him, firing several bursts, expending all my ammunition. During these bursts I saw a number of flashes on the fuselage and wings and a lot of smoke pouring out. Next, I saw his fuselage catch fire and he crashed to the ground and exploded'. Sqn Ldr Popławski used EN172 after replacing Sawicz as OC, whilst Capt Francis Gabreski also flew it with No 315 Sqn. In June 1943 the aircraft transferred to No 303 Sqn, where no fewer then seven aces used it on operations – Sqn Ldrs Rutkowski and Falkowski, Flt Lts Koc and Król, Plt Off Wünsche, Wt Off Popek and Flt Sgt Chudek. To the best of the authors' knowledge, this makes EN172 the most 'ace-flown' Spitfire in the PAF.

33

Spitfire IX LZ989 of Flt Lt Józef Jeka, No 316 Sqn, Northolt, August 1943

This Spitfire was Jeka's usual mount when he was 'A' Flight commander with No 316 Sqn. Indeed, it was in LZ989 that he achieved his final success, claiming an Fw 190 destroyed and another damaged on 19 August 1943. Other pilots to fly the Spitfire included aces Flt Lts Falkowski and Gnyś, Flg Off Maciejowski and Grp Capt Mümler (OC RAF Northolt at that time). Jeka had scored four and one shared kills with No 238 Sqn in the Battle of Britain, adding two confirmed victories to that score with No 306 Sqn. After the war he continued in his efforts to free Poland from Soviet rule, and to this end became involved in clandestine missions with the Americans. Jeka was apparently killed in a U-2 crash in the early 1950s.

34

Spitfire VIII JF447 of Sqn Ldr Stanisław 'Skal' Skalski, OC No 601 Sqn, Lentini West, August 1943

The practice of applying numbers to the more powerful Mk VIIIs and IXs (so as to differentiate them from the code letters worn by older Mk Vs) spread among the Mediterranean-based RAF units following its introduction by the PFT. JF447 was flown on several combat missions by Sqn Ldr Skalski (known as 'Skal' to his Commonwealth pilots), and typically for No 601 Sqn, the Spitfire carried its badge at the top of the fin. JF447 was an early Mk VIII, featuring a rounded rudder rather than the Mk XII-style broad-chord pointed variety. Interestingly, the rudder had a wire aerial attachment at the top, although HF radio sets were never fitted to Spitfire VIIIs.

35

Spitfire IX MA259 of Sqn Ldr Eugeniusz 'Horby' Horbaczewski, OC No 43 Sqn, Cassala, 4 September 1943

Horbaczewski took command of No 43 Sqn in August 1943, and subsequently flew MA259 just once – on 4 September 1943. The squadron ORB described the action of that day in the following extract; '15 aircraft were on patrol [in] Messina area. When formation was 10 miles East of Reggio 2 M.E. 109s were seen by the Spitfire IX section at 25,000 ft. approaching from the North East. Enemy aircraft turned North West and then seeing one aircraft opened fire on them and turned again to the North East diving vertically at very high speed. Our aircraft gave chase and one of the enemy aircraft was destroyed by S/Ldr. E. Horbaczewski (POL) at "deck level". Enemy aircraft crashed near Cittanova'.

36

Spitfire VC MA289 of Flt Lt Władysław 'Maciek' Drecki, No 152 Sqn, Milazzo East, 11 September 1943

The undersides of this Spitfire seem to have been painted in a lighter shade than the standard Azure Blue, the aircraft's original code letter (probably an A) having also been repainted. MA289 was usually flown by South African Harry Hoffe, although on 11 September Flt Lt Drecki borrowed it for the afternoon patrol over the Salerno beaches. During that mission he spotted a formation of USAAF P-38s being bounced by Bf 109s, and in a swift attack downed one of the fighters – probably that flown by Lt Rudolf Steffens of JG 53. This was No 152 Sqn's first kill after a barren spell, and it signalled the start of an eventful, and successful, period for the unit. Sadly, Drecki was killed in a take-off accident just 48 hours later.

37

Spitfire IX MK370 of Wg Cdr Julian 'Roch' Kowalski, Wing Leader No 131 (Polish) Fighter Wing, Chailey, May 1944

Immediately prior to D-Day the Luftwaffe offered little opposition to the marauding Allied air forces, so No 131 Wing's main task was the 'softening up' of German coastal defence in France – hence the white bomb markings on the cowling. Note the unusually low position of the wing commander's pennant. During May 1944 MK370 was also flown by Grp Capt Gabszewicz. Julian Kowalski was known throughout the PAF as 'Roch', after the character Roch Kowalski from a popular Polish novel. He had opened his score in France in June 1940 flying with GC I/145, and later joined No 302 Sqn and claimed a number of kills during the Battle of Britain.

38

Spitfire IX ML136 of Sqn Ldr Wacław Król, OC No 302 Sqn, Ford, summer 1944

It was customary in No 302 Sqn that the unit's OC flew an aeroplane coded WX-L 'for Leader'. This particular Spitfire was therefore used at the time by Sqn Ldr Król, who was known as 'the Monarch' – *król* means 'king' in Polish. By 1944 his score had reached its final total of eight and one shared kills. Interestingly, Król's first book of memoirs written after the war was entitled *My Spitfire WX-L*. ML136 was also flown by aces Wg Cdr Zumbach and Flt Lt Sołogub and Gnyś in mid-1944 – after Król left No 302 Sqn, the Spitfire was flown by Sqn Ldr Marian Duryasz. ML136 was destroyed on the ground on 1 January 1945 during the Luftwaffe's *Bodenplatte* attack on Ghent airfield.

39

Spitfire XVI TD317 of Sqn Ldr Karol Pniak, OC No 308 Sqn, Nordhorn, April 1945

TD317 was one of the few cut-down rear fuselage/tear-drop canopy Mk XVIs to reach PAF units before VE-Day – note the No 308 Sqn emblem below the windscreen. In accordance with 2nd TAF regulations, the Sky fuselage band and spinner have been repainted in darker shades so as to make the aeroplane less conspicuous when on the ground. Pniak scored two and one shared kills in 1939, and added a further four and one shared whilst with Nos 32 and 257 Sqns during 1940.

40

Mustang III FZ152 of Wg Cdr Stanisław Skalski, Wing Leader No 133 Wing, Coolham, May 1944

FZ152 was delivered to Coolham by Flt Lt Jeliński of No 306 Sqn on 8 April 1944, Skalski then using the Mustang until his departure from the wing in early August. During this time other pilots flew the aeroplane too, including aces Grp Capt Nowierski and Wt Off Wünsche (of No 315 Sqn). It was probably in FZ152 that Skalski was credited with two Bf 109s destroyed on 24 June 1944, apparently causing them to collide without firing a shot. The Mustang carried his full scoreboard and a personalised code of SS. It seems that Skalski originated the use of one's initials as personalised codes amongst PAF 'wingcos' with Spitfire IX BS556/S-S, which he had so marked after arriving at No 131 Wing in late 1943.

41

P-51B 43-6898 *The Deacon* of Maj Wacław (Winslow) 'Mike' Sobański, CO 334th FS/4th FG, Debden, May 1944

Sobański's personal aircraft were all coded QP-F. However, 'Mike' often used QP-J (especially after Nick Megura crash-landed P-51B 43-7158/QP-F in Sweden on 22 May), which was nominally assigned to Maj Howard Hively. Flying 43-6898, Sobański shared in the destruction of a Bf 110 over Lyon-Bron airfield on 30 April – the day the 4th FG claimed its 500th German aircraft destroyed. He was also flying *The Deacon* when he destroyed a Bf 109 on 28 May 1944 over Magdeburg. On D-Day Sobański used this P-51B in the afternoon mission that resulted in both him and his wingman being posted Missing In Action. 43-6898 was painted in standard USAAF camouflage of Olive Drab upper surfaces and Light Gray lower surfaces – just prior to D-Day the P-51B also received a full set of invasion stripes around the fuselage and wings. The Mustang carried Howard Hively's scoreboard of nine black crosses, and his personal emblem, *The Deacon*.

42

Mustang III FB145 of Flt Sgt Jakub Bargiełowski, No 315 Sqn, Coolham, May-June 1944

FB145 was ferried to No 315 Sqn from No 84 GSU on 13 April 1944 by Flt Sgt Bargiełowski, the pilot subsequently flying it regularly. On 12 June 1944 he opened his score with the Mustang III on a mission south of Caen at approximately 1240, four No 315 Sqn aircraft encountering seven Fw 190s. Sqn Ldr Horbaczewski and Flg Off Maciej Kirste each claimed a Focke-Wulf destroyed, while Bargiełowski downed two fighters. On 22 July 1944 FB145 was damaged in an accident, and never returned to No 315 Sqon.

43

Mustang III FB166 of Sqn Ldr Eugeniusz 'Dziubek' Horbaczewski, OC No 315 Sqn, Brenzett, June 1944

FB166 carries standard markings for that period, including invasion stripes, squadron badge and Polish square. Horbaczewski's tally included 12 black crosses with white outlines (kills) and 20 bombs (dive-bombing attacks). This aircraft had been ferried from Aston Down by Sgt Tamowicz on 13 April 1944, and subsequently became Horbaczewski's personal mount. On 12 June 'Dziubek' flew his Mustang fresh from an inspection at No 411 RSU and claimed an Fw 190 destroyed. The aeroplane was hit by flak during the same sortie, however, and returned directly to No 411 RSU for repair!

44

Mustang III FZ196 of Flt Lt Władysław Potocki, No 306 Sqn, Coolham, June 1944

On the evening of 7 June Potocki was flying UZ-D when he claimed two Bf 109s destroyed between Argentan and Caen. A cadet officer at Dęblin when war broke out, he eventually joined No 306 Sqn in 1942 and was credited with four and two shared German aircraft destroyed in 1944. By war's end Potocki was OC No 315 Sqn, and he then moved to No 309 Sqn. He subsequently completed a course at the Empire Test Pilots' School and went on to flight test the Avro Vulcan. Potocki then emigrated to Canada, where he worked for Avro Canada and tested the ill-fated CF-105 Arrow in 1959.

45

Mustang III HB886 of Grp Capt Tadeusz Nowierski, OC No 133 Wing, Brenzett, August 1944

Like most high-ranking officers at that time, Nowierski used his own initials as personalised codes. Otherwise, His Mustang carried standard markings, with D-Day stripes on the lower surfaces only in late summer 1944. Wg Cdr Rutkowski later used HB886 as KR. Nowierski had previously served with No 316 Sqn in 1941, before becoming OC No 308 Sqn in early 1942, and then being attached to the Northolt Wing HQ from mid-1942. In June 1943 he led the 2nd Polish Wing, and in October of that year assumed command of the wing, which had been re-numbered No 133 Wing as part of the 2nd TAF. He held this post until February 1945.

46

Mustang III FB353 of Flt Lt Longin Majewski, No 316 Sqn, Friston, August 1944

Although Flt Lt Majewski was not an ace in terms of enemy aircraft destroyed, he did, however, earn this title against 'doodlebugs'. His score stood at seven 'divers' (and a single Fw 190 shared) destroyed by the time he was assigned FB353, although his final V1 score was later downgraded to five and one shared. In late 1944 the fighter was transferred to No 315 Sqn, where it was flown as PK-H by squadron OC, Sqn Ldr Andersz – still carrying Majewski's scoreboard!

47

Mustang III HB868 of Wg Cdr Jan 'Johann' Zumbach, Wing Leader No 133 Wing, Brenzett, September 1944

Skalski's old friend, and rival, Zumbach took over No 133 Wing in the summer 1944. It is believed that 'Johann' flew this Mustang on 25 September when he was credited with an Fw 190 damaged – but for that one claim, his score had remained virtually unchanged since the days of EN951 *Donald Duck*. By 1944 Zumbach discontinued applying Disney motifs to his personal aircraft, although he still had his full scoreboard painted in colourful detail beneath the cockpit.

48

P-47D 42-25836 *PENGIE III* of Flt Lt Bolesław 'Mike' Gładych, 61st FS/56th FG, Boxted, May 1944

This P-47D was finished in standard USAAF natural metal, with unit markings in the form of a red band around the cowling and a red rudder. This was one in a sequence of so-named P-47s flown by Gładych, the previous aircraft (42-75140 *PENGIE II*) having been lost on 8 March during a mission in which 'Mike' downed an Fw 190, managed to escape the attentions of German ace Georg-Peter Eder and his wingman by leading them into German AA fire, and finally – with no fuel left – baled out over England. During August 42-25836 was replaced by 'bubbletop' P-47D 44-19718 *PENGIE IV*.

49

P-47D 42-26044 *Silver Lady* of Flt Lt Bolesław 'Mike' Gładych, 61st FS/56th FG, Boxted, July/August 1944

Although *Silver Lady* was the personal mount of Capt Leslie Smith, it was used frequently by Polish pilots. On 5 July Gładych shot down a Bf 109 with it and on 12 August claimed a Ju 88. 42-26044 was bare metal overall, and note the fitment of a Malcolm hood – a rare modification for a P-47. In the late summer of 1944 it carried worn D-Day stripes on its lower fuselage, plus standard red unit markings.

50

Mustang IVA KM112 of Sqn Ldr Bolesław 'Gandhi' Drobiński, OC No 303 Sqn, Coltishall, late 1945

KM112 was the OC's mount throughout No 303 Sqn's Mustang period. Peculiarly, its serial under the port wing was applied incorrectly as a mirror image. Like virtually all Mustang IVAs (P-51Ks), the aeroplane was bare metal overall with black codes. The Polish square was on the engine cowling and the unit badge positioned below the cockpit.

51

Mustang IV KH663 of Wt Off Jakub Bargiełowski, No 303 Sqn, Hethel, 1946

As part of the first batch of 30 Mark IVs (P-51Ds) delivered to the RAF, KH663 boasted a standard RAF temperate camouflage scheme, which was altogether non-standard on teardrop-canopied Mustangs in Britain. The aircraft featured the usual set of detail markings, with Sky codes and fuselage band, Polish square on the nose and the unit emblem beneath the canopy. Bargiełowski flew KH663 regularly during 1946, the Mustang also being flown by Wg Cdr Zumbach when he visited his old squadron.

FIGURE PLATES

1

Plut. Adolf Pietrasiak of *Escadrille Legere de Defence Ko* scored three shared kills with kpt. Kosiński's 'Chimney Flight' at Bourges in June 1940 – a score to which he would later add seven and one shared kills in Britain. He is wearing standard French pilot's gear. Note the seat-type parachute harness, one-piece overall and decidedly French headwear.

2

Destined to become one of the most successful pilots of the Polish and French campaigns (one and six shared kills plus four shared damaged), kpr. Jan Kremski served with *121 Eskadra* of the Cracow regiment. He is wearing a standard fighter pilot's summer flying suit, helmet and goggles. His black leather shoes were worn as standard, whilst his gloves appear to have been privately purchased.

3

One of top-scorers of the 1939 campaign, por. Wojciech Januszewicz took command of *111 Eskadra* after kpt. Gustaw Sidorowicz was wounded on 1 September. Januszewicz is wearing his dress uniform and standard fighter pilot's leather coat. His flying helmet and goggles are also regulation issue, although his rather colourful scarf is most definitely note!

4

By November 1941, No 317 Sqn's OC, Sqn Ldr Henryk 'Hesio' Szczęsny, boasted a score of six and three shared destroyed, one probable and two damaged. He would add two further kills on 4 April 1943, although the latter of these saw him collide with his target (an Fw 190), thus forcing him to bale out of his Spitfire Mk IX – he subsequently became a PoW. He is seen wearing a 1938 Pattern Irvin suit jacket over standard RAF Battle Dress and 1936 Pattern flying boots.

5

Known as 'Hrabia Oles' ('Sir Alec'), Gabszewicz commanded No 131 (Polish) Wing during late 1944. He is depicted wearing standard RAF Battle Dress, albeit with black shoes rather than flying boots. The tunic has a 'POLAND' shoulder flash and ribbons for his numerous decorations, which, by that time, included the Golden Cross of *Virtuti Militari* (the highest Polish decoration ever awarded to an airman – he was the first to receive it), the Silver Cross of *Virtuti Militari*, DSO and bar, DFC and bar, the *Krzyż Walecznych* (Cross of Valour) and three bars, and the *Croix de Guerre avec Palmes*. Beneath his tunic he is wearing a dark red scarf of No 316 Sqn.

6

Polish top-scorer of the French campaign, Sgt Eugeniusz Nowakiewicz later added to his tally flying with No 302 Sqn. He is seen wearing a Battle Dress tunic (note the 'POLAND' flash on his shoulder above the rank emblem) over a standard RAF issue light blue shirt and black tie, combined rather unusually with 1938 Pattern Irvin suit trousers and black leather shoes!

ACKNOWLEDGEMENTS

The publication of this book would not have been possible without the help of Polish and Allied veterans – and their families – who shared with us their memories and archives (they will forgive us listing their names alphabetically rather than by rank); Beryl Arct (widow of the late Bohdan Arct), Jakub Bargiełowski, Stanislaw Bochniak, Michał Cwynar, Bolesław Gładych, Czesław Główczyński, James Goodson, Jack Ilfrey, Edward Jaworski, Bolesław Jedliczko, Thomas E Johnson, J Norby King (who allowed us to quote passages from his book, *Green Kiwi Versus German Eagle - The Journal of a New Zealand Fighter Pilot*, New Zealand 1991), Wojciech Kołączkowski, Charles Konsler, Piotr Kuryłłowicz, Donald S Lopez, W J Malone, Ludwik Martel, W M Matheson, Eric H Moore, Bożydar Nowosielski, Ignacy Olszewski, Witold Pomarański, Tom Ross, Tadeusz Sawicz, the late Ian Shand, Frank Speer, Tadeusz Szlenkier, Jerzy Szymankiewicz, John Tilston, Jack Torrance, Marian Trzebiński, the late Witold Urbanowicz, *Stanislaw* Wandzilak and the late Stefan Witorzeńć.

Our research into the subject of Polish aces was inspired years ago by Józef Zieliński and Dr Alfred Price. Whilst working on the subject we have received continuous support from Jerzy B Cynk, which has proved to be invaluable for he was working at the same time on his fundamental work about the Polish Air Force in World War 2 (it is noteworthy that Mr Cynk's pioneering *History of the Polish Air Force 1918-1968* was published 26 years ago by Osprey), which is due to be published in 1998. We also received invaluable assistance from Krzysztof Chołoniewski, an expert in Polish Air Force aircraft serials and codes, and from Andrzej Suchcitz of the Polish Institute and Sikorski Museum in London. Several chapters of this book appear with substantial assistance from our friends, whose names can be found at the start of the relevant sections (which by no means implies that their help was limited to these respective chapters alone). Other good friends provided information of a more general nature, or made available documents or photographs of special value. Thank you to Peter R Arnold, Donald L Caldwell, Stefan Czmur, Seweryn Fleischer, Franciszek Ksawery Grabowski, Mariusz Gronostaj, Dr Jan P Koniarek, Tomasz Kopański, Wojciech Łuczak, Jerzy Pawlak, Michael Payne, Thomas Rajkowski, Pawel Sembrat, Christopher Shores, Robert Stachyra, Olivier Tyrbas, Krzysztof Wagner, Grzegorz Zaleski, Mariusz Zimny, the staff of *IV Liceum Ogólnokształcace im. kpt. E. Horbaczewskiego* in Zielona Góra, and especially to the tireless Mrs Maria Tarnowska.

Finally, we would like to acknowledge Robert 'Buba' Grudzień, who produced all the Spitfire profiles for this book. His efforts to prepare accurate scale drawings, and subseqently his research into actual camouflage/marking combinations, have proven to be invaluable.